Drama
for All

For Jesse,
. . . his teachers, and beginners in drama everywhere!

Drama
for All

**Developing drama
in the curriculum
with pupils with
special educational
needs**

Melanie Peter

David Fulton Publishers
London

David Fulton Publishers Ltd
2 Barbon Close, London WC1N 3JX

First published in Great Britain by
David Fulton Publishers 1994
Reprinted 1995

Note: The right of Melanie Peter to be identified as the author of this work has been asserted by her in accordance with the Copyright, Designs and Patents Act 1988.

British Library Cataloguing in Publication Data
A catalogue record for this book is available from the British Library

ISBN 1-85346-315-9

Typeset by Franklin Graphics, Southport

Printed in Great Britain by Bell and Bain Ltd, Glasgow

Contents

Acknowledgements

First of all, my thanks and appreciation must go to all staff and pupils with whom I have worked – this handbook would not exist without them. Two headteachers, Pat Mathias and Tom Howard, and Howard Reid (former Drama Adviser for Norfolk LEA) have been particularly encouraging in facilitating opportunities for me to develop my practice in the arts and special needs. I thank them for their enthusiasm and support.

I am grateful to John Taylor, former Advisory Teacher in the Inner London Education Authority, for the prototype for the diagrams on pages 10 and 12, for his permission to reproduce some of his drama activities on pages 56 to 63 (see page 56), for prompting some of my thinking for the lessons on pages 66, 74, 76 and 82 . . . and for his innovation! I am also indebted to two other notable influences. Firstly, Veronica Sherborne, my former tutor on my PGCE in Bristol, for her inspirational approach to creativity within an educational context with pupils with special educational needs. Secondly, David Sheppard, my former tutor on the RSA Diploma in drama in education, for his encouragement and support in my endeavours to apply mainstream principles for drama teaching to pupils with special educational needs.

I wish to thank Jim Clark (Senior Lecturer in Arts in Education, University of Northumbria at Newcastle), and Judy Sebba (Tutor in Special Educational Needs, University of Cambridge Institute of Education) for their advice in putting this handbook together. Lastly, but by no means least, I extend a heartfelt thank you to my family, for their patience and encouragement, especially whilst I have been writing it all up!

Introduction

This handbook is endeavouring to bridge a gap between the fields of special educational needs and drama-in-education (classroom drama as opposed to drama for performance) – very little in fact has been documented in this area in recent years. It is written with two groups of people in mind, who represent perhaps opposite ends of a continuum: those teachers of pupils with special educational needs wishing to venture into drama, and those mainstream drama practitioners wishing to develop their work with pupils with special educational needs. *Drama for All* offers a practical approach to drama-in-education based on current mainstream theory and practice, that is accessible to *all* beginners in drama – staff as well as pupils – and which embraces those students with severe and moderate learning disabilities as well as those with emotional and behavioural difficulties.

Drama with pupils with special educational needs has lagged behind curriculum development generally in special education, and behind developments in mainstream practice in drama-in-education. Following Warnock, the 1980s saw the growth of a rigorous definition of curriculum content in special education, with the emphasis on the acquisition of clearly-observable skills, broken down into small achievable steps; finely tuned behavioural approaches to teaching became popular. For many teachers (and pupils too, no doubt), drama seemed 'light relief' from intensive learning programmes elsewhere in the curriculum, and offered opportunities to balance individual teaching with group work.

Nevertheless, many teachers have felt incompetent or uneasy in drama with pupils with special educational needs. This is partly attributable to the influence of the Remedial Drama and Dramatherapy movement in the 1970s and 1980s, which demonstrated the power of drama for 'helping and healing', and where the definition of what constituted drama was kept necessarily vague. Teachers have been uncertain over using drama, and, recognizing the power of drama, reluctant to expose their pupils if they inadvertently 'took the lid off something'. The upshot is that much drama activity in the hands of *teachers* (as opposed to dramatherapists with a different agenda) with pupils with special educational needs has tended to be fairly superficial and ad hoc. Drama games have been used to promote the 'social health' of a group; role-play simulations have been used to practise social skills (eg, making a phone call); stories have been brought to life through reenactment by the pupils; or else their make-believe play has been expanded into a more elaborate improvised narrative. The potential of using drama as a learning medium and teaching methodology however, has been little explored with pupils with special educational needs – that is, where the teacher *challenges* the participants' make-believe in order to deepen understanding and to offer a change in insight through spontaneous role-taking.

Drama for All seeks to offer practitioners a developmental approach to drama-in-education with pupils with special educational needs that is compatible with mainstream practice, and a 'thought process' for structuring drama in a way that will increasingly challenge all the participants. It aims to enable all students to learn from the power of drama's 'double edge' as described by Gavin Bolton (1984), doing drama but with the *awareness* of doing it at the same time: consenting to and being involved in creating and experiencing the make-believe, in the safety of it being 'one step removed'. Compare this with the approach commonly adopted by many theatre-in-education groups working in this field, where heavily in role from the outset, they greet the children with 'Hi! I'm from outer space. . .'. 'Oh, hello', often comes the bland reply – for these pupils with learning difficulties, this may not represent an extension of their experience at all, but seem just part of everyday life; what the pupils are missing here is the opportunity to gain an objective angle on themselves and their behaviour.

Drama for All proposes a framework for one approach in drama for all pupils. However, consideration is given to the particular adaptations and modifications needed to accommodate the pressures and demands when working in this particularly challenging field. Useful teaching strategies are discussed, with a further chapter devoted to coping with particular management difficulties that may arise. A substantial appendix offers ideas and examples of lessons carried out in a range of provision for pupils with differing special educational needs. Many of the lessons are drawn from my experience as a primary Drama Advisory Teacher for Norfolk LEA between Autumn 1991 and Spring 1992, when I was seconded from my post as the creative arts teacher in an SLD school, with the brief of developing drama with pupils with special educational needs across a range of provision. I should add that the same approach to drama may be used with secondary-age pupils. In fact, I have carried out many of the lessons with senior age pupils too across the ability range, although in some cases, ideas have needed adapting in order to make the content sophisticated and age-appropriate for older students.

From teachers' comments, both during this project and elsewhere, time and again it is their lack of confidence in having a structure – knowing how to begin and develop drama, not just lack of ideas – that they perceive as their stumbling block, particularly given the idiosyncrasies of their pupils with special educational needs and the particular challenges of very mixed-ability teaching. This handbook will attempt therefore to provide a *framework for drama:* to elucidate the drama process, to explain steps into drama and how to build the drama, if necessary in very small increments, whether for the benefit of the pupils or indeed the teachers, or both, in developing confidence in understanding and using the drama medium for learning and to communicate ideas. This grasp of the drama process is fundamental, the key to all drama and theatre work.

Achievement in educational drama may not necessarily be age or ability related: whilst lacking in actual worldliness, a 6-year-old even with severe learning difficulties may have more drama *savoir faire* and be more able to use the medium and work within the art form than a mainstream adolescent. Likewise, a pupil with special educational needs may not necessarily be disadvantaged in drama alongside a mainstream peer – significant for integration practices. Therefore, whilst this handbook has been aimed particularly at those working with pupils with learning difficulties, it is hoped that practitioners in all phases of education, whether experienced or inexperienced in drama, will also find interest and relevance in *Drama for All.*

CHAPTER 1

Contemplating the Challenge – drama in the curriculum in relation to pupils with special educational needs

This chapter will first of all place drama in the curriculum offered to pupils with special educational needs, before considering the relationship between drama in the mainstream of education and drama for pupils with special educational needs, essentially by examining what is drama-in-education. Is it the case that there is one kind of drama suitable for pupils with special educational needs and another kind for mainstream pupils? Some of the issues will be tackled and the challenges confronted, that this question necessarily begs with regard to approaching and planning for drama with pupils with special educational needs.

Drama in Context

• Whilst drama is not a foundation subject within the National Curriculum, it is identified as part of the statutory core subject of English, with a specific contribution to the development of speaking and listening skills.

• Drama's power as a potent teaching style is recognized within Orders across the curriculum, notably science, technology, history and modern foreign languages.

• Cross-curricular dimensions, skills and themes that comprise the wider 'whole curriculum' beyond the core and foundation subjects incorporate many aspects of personal and social education, such as problem solving, education for citizenship, equal opportunities and multicultural education. Traditionally, such issues have provided the content for drama-in-education, where drama is used as a learning medium to deepen understanding and bring about a change in insight. Commonly, these areas are also identified by special schools as key aims and objectives for their students, where it is recognized that they may need to be explicitly taught.

✳ The point is, that although drama is not regarded as a separate foundation subject in the National Curriculum, its value as a teaching tool is recognized. This is further endorsed by the consideration given to drama in the OFSTED framework for the inspection of schools (1992). Specifically, 'speaking and listening' extends across all curriculum areas, and is a key factor by which inspection teams judge standards of achievement. Where drama can be viewed in its own right, OFSTED proposes that it should be considered under the same two-part framework as Art and Music:

- creating and performing drama;
- appreciating and appraising it.

Thus, all drama work with pupils with special educational needs can be seen as having direct bearing on National Curriculum implementation.

Drama and Language Development

The contribution of drama to the development of language deserves elaboration and indeed probably merits a book to itself. Drama is considered integral to the development of communication, and for promoting speaking and listening skills (NCC, 1990). Certain key points, with their particular relevance to pupils with special educational needs, need to made here:

- **Symbolic understanding** – the teacher may have to support the spoken word with real objects or picture material according to a pupil's level of conceptual development. It may be that drama offers an opportunity to extend the pupil's symbolic understanding by gradually replacing real objects and props with more representational imagery (toys, miniature objects, photos, pictures), working towards the unsupported spoken and written word. Likewise, the same prop may be used flexibly and with a variety of representational functions (eg, a table to be a bed, cave, rock, etc.).
- **Vocabulary** – drama offers opportunities to introduce vocabulary naturally in context, where the pupil can learn the use and meaning in relation to his or her behaviour in situations where he or she is physically active and his or her attention is engaged.
- **Articulation** – drama offers opportunities to work on certain speech sounds in a motivating and less pressured way, for example 'sssshhh . . . sssssshhh . . .', the sound of wind in the trees, possibly as a soundscape in the unfolding drama.
- **Accuracy** – drama may be contrived so that the pupil finds a need/sense of urgency or reason to use a particular construction or aspect of language correctly in order to obtain something, whilst the use of role protects the child from the consequences of inaccuracy as it is happening in a make-believe context. For example, a message incorrectly delivered in the drama may lead to untoward consequences, thus demonstrating the effect of inaccuracy. (It may be possible to practise the necessary linguistic skills, or re-do the particular scene if necessary.) In this way, the pupils may be led to discover the importance of accuracy in both speaking and listening.
- **Conversational competence** – these are subtleties of interaction that may need to be explicitly emphasized with pupils with special educational needs. Drama offers opportunities to develop what is relevant in

conversation, and to explore and inhibit inappropriate contributions in the safety of this happening one step removed. Relevant aspects include appropriate comments, turn-taking skills, organizing ideas logically and concisely, socially appropriate body language, etc. For example, a teacher in role may be legitimately irritated at a hesitant mumbling response, so impelling the pupil (in role) to find a more appropriate manner.

• **Oracy** – selecting the form of a message and language used according to audience, situation and purpose. Different contexts offered in drama challenge the pupils with new language demands. Drama can empower pupils by bringing in to the 'here and now' the relationship between communication skills and its effect on others. For example, a teacher in a high status authority role may demand formal skills of address from the pupils (in role), before consenting to give them an audience.

• **Literacy** – development of speaking and listening skills may influence pupils' literacy. Drama may also provide a meaningful context to write in a particular linguistic style and to read and interpret visual and written material in context. Drama may motivate writing as a means to reflect on and follow up an experience.

The Value of Drama in the Curriculum

The place and importance of drama in the curriculum for pupils with special educational needs may be summarized in the following points:

→ • **Balancing** highly-structured, individual teaching situations, with the emphasis on the group.

• **Serving** cross-curricular learning, by giving a reason and sense of urgency to use skills, concepts and factual knowledge, and to generalize and practise skills in context, eg, language, self-help skills, etc.

→ • **Facilitating** opportunities for creating many different possible contexts in which to assess pupils' learning in situations that are necessarily less pressured and more natural, so enabling a more realistic indication of pupils' abilities.

→ • **Developing** a sense of inner resourcefulness in pupils to apply learning (very important for pupils with special educational needs), as well as critical thought, discrimination and a sense of enquiry.

→ • **Complementing** an essentially skill-based curriculum, in providing opportunities within the 'whole curriculum' for a unique kind of learning: personal and social development as part of a group, and deepening understanding and awareness of attitudes and issues, and insight into why people think and behave as they do.

• **Accessing** areas of the curriculum, including previously uncharted areas of the National Curriculum (eg, modern foreign languages, history, geography) to pupils with special eduational needs by 'bringing them to life' – active learning par excellence.

• **Enriching** an essentially skill-based curriculum, by focusing on topics and themes, and providing a meaningful context to pupils in which to integrate knowledge, concepts and skills.

→ • **Empowering** pupils by offering rich opportunities for language development, particularly consideration of audience, context and social purpose in language use in a variety of situations.

→   • **Enabling** pupils to become more independent learners and to take responsibility for their own learning, through opportunities to identify their learning needs in process – this bargaining and negotiation between teacher and pupils is central to the drama process.

→   • **Raising** self-esteem through fun and satisfaction from the drama form – understanding and using the drama medium to share and explore human experience, and to express and communicate ideas in an analogous life situation.

One Drama for All?

The 1981 Warnock Act set an ideological stamp on developing integration practices and mixed-ability teaching. The teacher of drama, now more than ever, needs to be able to differentiate his/her teaching to work with pupils of any ability, whether in a mainstream or special school situation. It needs to be stated here, that in any case, pupils of similar chronological age may be at the same level of emotional maturity, whether or not they are deemed to have 'special educational needs'. Such positive disposition towards pupils with special educational needs may now be under threat: with LMS funding linked per capita to the most popular schools (likely to be regarded as those achieving in National Curriculum tests), even well-intentioned governing bodies may be tempted to underplay provision for pupils with special educational needs. Nevertheless, it is important that teachers of drama working in all phases of education are able to evaluate their work by the same criteria, and draw from the resource materials available in drama.

How can it be, though, that one kind of drama can suit *all* pupils in *all* situations, given the differing needs of pupils in all phases of the education system? How can 'special needs drama' and 'mainstream drama' necessarily be 'the same but different'? John Taylor (1986a, p.17) analyses the relationship through a useful analogy borrowed from linguistics:

> . . . in terms of its *deep structure* the drama lesson has certain essential elements, detectable in lessons at every level of learning. In terms of its *surface structure*, however, it is immensely flexible. For while the deep structure concerns the very dynamic of the drama process, its principle of operation, the surface structure is about tactics and strategies, the things a teacher sets up in a lesson in order for the principles to be worked through.

In other words, whilst the underlying *drama process* may remain fundamentally the same, the difference from lesson to lesson in the choice of *drama conventions* (ways to organize the drama) will vary as meaning is negotiated and created between the participants. Learning will take place when the pupils experience the relationship between the drama form and the content of the drama, which may become highly skilled and crafted and increasingly sophisticated as the pupils progress in their ability to understand and use drama as a learning medium. Learning about and learning through drama are therefore essentially interrelated activities; this relationship obtains in all drama activity at all levels of sophistication.

4

The Drama Process

Drama-in-education has metamorphosed considerably in recent years. It has now come to mean something other than theatre skills, improvisation, role-play or performance. So what is classroom drama as currently practised in schools? . . . What is the difference between drama and 'make-believe play', such as that in the playground or home-corner? . . . Imagine a playground scenario where children are playing at underwater explorers . . . swiftly they invent a helicopter to get out of a fix. . . . An easy solution enables the momentum to be sustained and the story-line to unfold. The drama teacher however, would put the brakes on '. . .wait a minute' . . . and endeavour to make the pupils consider the implications of their suggestions and work at resolving the situation, giving their 'play' structure in process.

The drama teacher, then, is looking to reach a point where he or she can *challenge make-believe play* to create potential areas of learning, and lead the pupils to explore these through the use of a range of drama conventions which give shape and structure to the elements of dramatic form (the drama teacher's 'tools' – to be expanded on more fully in Chapter 5). The unfolding drama is really on two levels: the 'play for the pupils', and the 'play for the teacher' as coined by Geoff Gilham (1974), with the teacher harnessing the pupils' make-believe play, and seeking to set up situations for the pupils to reflect on their behaviour, ideas and feelings through active identification with the fictitious situation. Pupils are encouraged to discover the implications of their behaviour in the safety of it being 'one-step-removed' through the use of role, and are empowered to take responsibility for their own learning. Indeed, the position of 'teacher' shifts from the conventional teacher:pupil relationship, which is particularly significant for many pupils with special educational needs, given their usual highly-structured and more didactic teaching situations.

John Taylor (1986a, p.18) uses a vivid metaphor and likens the drama process to the idea of Frankenstein's monster, a created thing that somehow turns on its creator:

> . . . educational drama has the following object – to get participants so caught up in the thick of a make-believe experience that at a certain point the fiction appears to become, in some sense, independent of its creators and to exert upon them forces which confront and challenge them. This switch-around need not necessarily manifest itself as a crisis or a shocking event, but it will always involve the transfer, gradual or sudden, from a phase in which the participants are shaping and influencing the fiction to a phase where they are permitting the fiction to shape and influence them.

To summarize

Drama-in-education is:

- a method of enquiry;
- a motivating force, capitalizing on children's play;
- a means for personal and social development; and
- a teaching method

5

which uses conventions of the dramatic art form, to enable pupils to understand themselves and their world, to consider why people think and behave as they do.

How can pupils with special educational needs be enabled to learn in and through drama in the way described in this chapter? Let's meet the challenge . . . .

CHAPTER 2

Meeting the Challenge – approaching and planning for drama with pupils with special educational needs

The prospect of doing drama with pupils with special educational needs can seem daunting for a variety of reasons, not least because many practitioners working in this field will be non-specialist teachers of drama. This chapter will begin to explore a framework for drama with pupils with special educational needs that is developmental for the teacher as much as for the pupils – learning how to do drama whilst doing it!

Approaching Drama with Pupils with Special Educational Needs

Difficulties in drama for the teacher

Many pupils with sensory or physical disabilities may well be capable of engaging in the same sort of drama as their able-bodied peers, although presenting logistical challenges to the teacher to enable them to participate fully. However, the teacher contemplating drama with pupils with learning disabilities or emotional and behavioural difficulties may face particular problems.

- **Empowering the pupils:** especially those with limited verbal powers of expression and sensory disabilities.
- **Reorientation in planning:** drama focuses on developing the group's attitudes, issues and understanding – considering what people have in common, rather than planning for individual differences in skill-based activities, as elsewhere in the curriculum.
- **Additional staff:** planning for classroom assistant(s) and/or supporting professionals – maximizing the resource.
- **Pressures of timetabling:** planning within the constraints of a shorter school day – many pupils with special educational needs are 'bussed' in and have considerable requirements in terms of speech/physio/music therapies, toileting at regular intervals, etc.
- **Confidence in handling less-structured activity:** drama is creative and open-ended, handing over decisions to the pupils, unlike the highly-structured behavioural teaching approaches often favoured in special education.

• **Lassitude in evaluation:** the outcome of a lesson in terms of learning may not always be readily or immediately identifiable, unlike a clearly observable skill.

• **Extreme range of abilities:** it is not uncommon to find a range of mental ages, from 6 months to 7 years, within the same group.

• **Motivating the group:** establishing a 'collective agreement' for the drama, especially with an extreme range of abilities.

• **Idiosyncratic responses:** this can present difficulties in balancing individual and group needs, and demand skill in making responses relevant and appropriate, and in converting pupils' initiatives almost instantaneously into worthwhile learning experiences.

• **Unpredictability of the pupils:** both their responses in the drama and their behaviour which may present management challenges.

• **'Thinking on one's feet':** most likely the teacher will not have the option of using strategies that might give a few moments' 'thinking time', because of the pupils' relative inability to set themselves imaginary goals and sustain the make-believe independently.

• **Being on one's mettle:** the pupils may be relatively unable to take over the leadership of the drama as quickly or as smoothly as their mainstream peers.

• **Limited worldliness of the pupils:** a limited range of experiences on which to draw.

• **Working from the interests of the group:** the teacher may risk losing them altogether if not, as the pupils may not have the mental agility to consider alternatives, a point made by Dorothy Heathcote. It can be little or no comfort to read that Dorothy Heathcote (in Wagner, 1976, p.210) urged her student teachers to work with children with severe learning difficulties

> . . . because the pressure they provide is a good proving ground for any teacher of any group. With the mentally-handicapped, you have to rely more on what you are than on what you know.

Difficulties in drama for the pupils

The greatest difficulty facing the teacher of drama with many pupils with special educational needs, concerns the actual nature of drama itself. Essentially, the whole thing hinges on make-believe play: the core of the drama process. For various reasons, this is problematic for many pupils with special educational needs.

Pupils are likely to be at different levels of conceptual and social development in terms of their make-believe play and symbolic understanding:

• pupils developmentally may not have reached the point where they have grasped the concept of symbolism and make-believe;

• pupils may be developmentally ready and able to join in make-believe play, but may not spontaneously play in this way – they may lack the drive or ability to set imaginary goals and sustain them;

• pupils may lack security and/or the necessary social skills to engage in make-believe as part of a group.

The drama teacher therefore will need to find ways to *enable* pupils with differing special educational needs within a mixed-ability group to develop the necessary conceptual understanding and interaction skills to engage in make-believe as part of the group. As suggested above however, *learning about and learning through drama should be considered an on-going process*, from drama in the nursery classroom to a production at the Royal National Theatre. Nevertheless, certain groundwork in gaining a 'handle' on the drama medium may be achieved more directly by gradually empowering the pupils to make choices and decisions. Paradoxically, by *limiting* choices and decisions, this may actually *enable* pupils to create and engage in divergent thinking. What it comes down to is planning drama activity in a differentiated way for pupils at differing levels of conceptual and social development, whilst retaining the essence of the drama process so that, at their respective ability levels, they are able to learn in and through drama. In other words, doing drama and learning how to do drama at the same time!

Planning for Drama with Pupils with Special Educational Needs

A drama lesson will always be a combination of pupil input and teacher input. The ratio will depend on:

- the teacher's own confidence and experience in drama;
- the experience and confidence of the class in drama, and the teacher's perception of their need for a new challenge;
- the particular ideas the teacher wants to explore, or experiences he or she wants the class to have.

At first glance, planning drama may seem to contradict the notion of maximizing pupils' decision-making and creativity. However, many pupils with special educational needs in particular may need considerable help in discovering their autonomy and in enabling them to be empowered effectively. The teacher of drama can have a *range of options along a drama continuum*, whereby choices and decisions can be paced and gradually handed over to the pupils. It may be that a particular group of pupils with special educational needs may present at a broadly similar level of development in their potential for understanding and using drama as a learning medium. It may be the case, then, that a particular type of drama activity is appropriate for all of them. In my experience however, this is not often the case! Usually, the teacher is having to cater for a range of special educational needs within a group. Drama is a group activity: there should be no reason for anyone to be excluded. However, in practical terms, this does mean that the drama will have to be structured to reach 'all the people *some* of the time', if not 'all the people *all* the time'.

First of all however, it is helpful to be aware of a progression in terms of drama activity, where 'ownership of the drama' may be gradually handed over to the pupils. Let us look more closely at this notion of a 'drama continuum'. John Taylor (1984) originally advocated this developmental approach to drama, not based on any concept of necessary child developmental stages of learning, but rather representing an *order*

9

of teaching, beneficial for both teacher and pupil for 'learning the language of drama'.

A Drama continuum

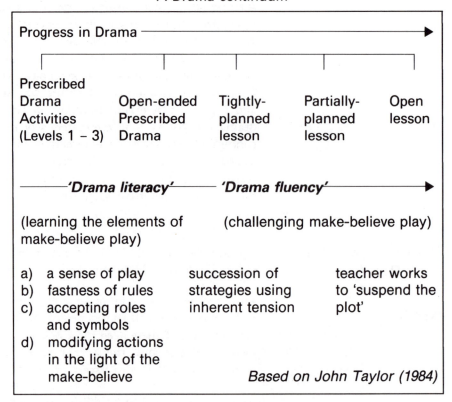

As John Taylor pointed out (1984), it is not so much that the pupils may require a developmental approach to drama, but rather that the teacher may, in order to acquire practice in using drama conventions and strategies, so as to be able ultimately to convert those decisions and choices the pupils make as the lesson proceeds into worthwhile learning experiences. The incidental spin-off from the teacher's increasing confidence will be security for the group in engaging in ostensibly less-structured activity. Furthermore, as indicated above, it is a feature of many children with special educational needs, that even when they may be developmentally ready to join in make-believe play, frequently they do not spontaneously play in this way. As Gavin Bolton has noted (1979), a teaching aim, albeit at a subsidiary level, must be for pupils to acquire the basic drama/theatre skills of selecting focus, injecting tension and creating meaningful symbols. For pupils with special educational needs however, this may have to be at an even more basic level.

To this end, John Taylor devised his own brand of drama activities which he called 'Drama Games'. The term 'drama game' more usually refers to a relatively superficial energizer or warm-up activity, to concentrate attention and establish 'the group'. John Taylor's 'Drama Games' differ significantly however, in that the make-believe context is crucial from the outset, so that the participants are necessarily caught up in the pretence. They are also carefully structured, so that active involvement within the make-believe can be paced and closely monitored. In this way, doing drama and learning how to do drama become part of the same process. The teacher and pupil can progressively 'learn the language of drama' (the elements of make-believe play for drama – *drama literacy*), and choices can be increasingly handed over to the pupils. To avoid misconception therefore, I prefer to term such activities as 'Prescribed Drama Structures' (see Chapter 3) in the sense of the tightness of planning and of delivery of the activity, although there will be opportunity for pupil choice and decision-making within the structure. These represent one end of the drama continuum.

Once the pupils are playing freely within the make-believe in open-ended Prescribed Drama Structures, and are handling choices and decisions as a group within the make-believe, they are ready to have their play challenged. At the other end of the drama continuum then, is the kind of drama activity recognized by mainstream practitioners but, I would maintain, no less within the grasp of many teachers and pupils within special education, whereby the pupils' make-believe play is challenged and 'play taken into learning' – potential areas of learning explored: using drama as a learning medium – *drama fluency*.

It may be that not all pupils in a very mixed-ability group will have reached this point: for them, it will be important to ensure that a Prescribed Drama Structure is contextualized at some point in an open-ended drama, so that they may continue developing their conceptual understanding of make-believe. However, provided that the majority of the group is 'ready' for more open-ended work, there is no reason why all the pupils in the group may not continue the process of doing drama and learning how to do drama at the same time. For most, this will mean developing skills in handling more sophisticated forms of dramatic expression and making meaning in drama, whilst the others will be continuing to learn the basic elements of make-believe. Both may continue to develop within the framework of open-ended drama.

The next chapter will begin to consider planning for drama with pupils with special educational needs in greater depth. The elements of make-believe involved in drama will be examined more closely, and how these can be usefully fostered and developed in Prescribed Drama Strucures, which may become increasingly *less* prescribed, with the aim of achieving 'drama literacy' (understanding of the drama medium), and ultimately 'drama fluency' (use of the medium of drama for learning).

A RANGE OF OPTIONS FOR PLANNING DRAMA:

Type of activity	*Structure*
Prescribed Dramas	Activities are prescribed by rules of procedure. They can progressively hand over more and more choices to the pupils within the teacher's structure:
level 1 –	– limited physical or verbal response;
level 2 –	– physical but not verbal response required;
level 3 –	– conceptually more demanding, often requiring a verbal response.
'Open-ended' Prescribed Drama	Activities are prescribed up to a point, but lead towards a moment when pupils are allowed some sort of free decision, maybe even supplying a solution to problems which change the drama, eg, 'How can we get our ball back?'
Tightly-planned drama lesson (linear model)	Teacher plans in advance what the component activities of the lesson will be, but the pupils have freedom within each activity. NB: the teacher should still be on the look-out for pupil interests and other learning areas that may arise, and be prepared to abandon the original plan.
Partially-planned drama lesson	Teacher plans possible opening (roles, place, focus or problem) and has in mind several possible developments with predetermined conventions (a number of successive conventions are possible). Teacher is on the look-out for possible learning areas, so that the outcome remains flexible.
'Open' drama lesson	The pupils are invited to make crucial decisions from the outset: topic for the drama, roles, place and action, are all negotiated. Teacher watches for the way the pupils seem to want the drama to go, and diagnoses their learning need. Teacher uses a number of drama conventions to make pupils work at achieving goals.

Adapted from John Taylor (1984)

CHAPTER 3

'Drama Literacy' – towards understanding drama

This chapter will endeavour to get down to the nitty gritty: to put under the microscope the notion of 'doing drama and learning how to do drama' all at the same time. In the last chapter, I suggested that perhaps the biggest stumbling block to developing drama with pupils with special educational needs was that the whole thing hinged on make-believe play; for various reasons, pupils with special educational needs may have difficulty with this. However, as Gavin Bolton (1992, p.114) comments:

> It is the teacher's responsibility, no matter how young the children are, to foster a sense of theatre which they may or may not be able to articulate. . . . This simple knowledge of the 'game of theatre' is something that drama classes must understand and appreciate as soon as possible, and teachers should continually be alert to opportunities for teaching that game.

This chapter will describe how it is possible to teach that 'game of theatre'. It will look at becoming 'drama literate': learning the 'language of drama' – the elements of make-believe – whilst actually engaged within a fictitious drama context from the very outset. It will consider using Prescribed Drama activities where the 'game of theatre' is clearly defined. This type of activity can be used complete in itself, but may also be used flexibly as a core pivot activity, a basis for leading a group into making progressively more open-ended choices and decisions in drama, however long that process might take. In this way, teacher and pupils can take themselves gradually along the continuum into increasingly more open-ended drama.

Learning about Make-believe

When a young baby first discovers pretence, it is very often in the following kind of situation: baby throws rattle out of cot – parent feigns anger at baby – baby does it again . . . and again, and again, and again. The whole pretence becomes ritualized. What the baby is checking out is whether this 'suspension of disbelief', the pretence, can be repeated, and discovering his or her power to generate and sustain that pretence within a secure, familiar structure. In essence, it is this kind experience that needs to be captured in drama – the 'game of theatre'. It is for this reason that I

13

propose development in drama initially through Prescribed Drama activities (originally formulated and termed 'Drama Games' by John Taylor, 1983), as they offer a secure framework where ritualized pretence can be discovered and explored. Incidental spin-offs from the turn-taking format will be training in group-work, and increasing confidence of staff and pupils in negotiating within the make-believe.

Prescribed Drama activities will enable the pupil to 'gain a handle' and understand the essential elements of drama, whilst progressively taking over the choices and decisions within the make-believe. The engagement of the pupils can be paced and closely monitored. This type of activity involves pupils from the outset in pretence: even at a most basic level, role is used, so that all participants are necessarily caught up in make-believe. Whilst not to be confused with a 'drama game' in the sense of a superficial warm-up activity, a Prescribed Drama Structure makes the 'game of theatre' explicit, and has a clear 'game' framework at its core.

All Prescribed Drama activities are necessarily limited in their usefulness as a vehicle for learning, and do *not* represent the scope and power of drama as a learning medium, for challenging pupils' attitudes, ideas and preconceptions about themselves and the world in which they live as revealed in their make-believe play. They have a fixed structure, and are complete in themselves with a clear beginning-middle-end; they are repetitive, involving ritualistic turn-taking. Their tight structure, therefore, tends to limit innovation and initiative. *However, they are useful starting points:*

- for a teacher to gain confidence and practice in using drama conventions, including working in role;
- as valuable training in group-work in an ostensibly less-structured type of activity – security for certain pupils and also security for the teacher;
- for teaching pupils the essential elements of drama:
  - **a sense of play** – an emerging awareness of make-believe;
  - **fastness of rules** – everyone to 'play the game', in order to sustain the make-believe;
  - **accepting roles and symbols** – consenting to the make-believe, not being deluded into it;
  - **modifying actions in the light of the make-believe** – adapting their own behaviour in response to the drama.

Features of Prescribed Drama Structures

In style, this kind of activity resembles a game: turn-taking, a clearly defined beginning-middle-end, and complete in itself. It involves elements of cross-curricular learning, and has a crucial 'as if' make-believe context, so that the participants are caught up in pretence from the outset. In this way, the pupils can begin to grasp the 'game of theatre'. The following elements may be used as pointers for devising your own Prescribed Drama activities to meet the specific needs of your teaching group.

- **An element of make-believe**: this helps motivate staff as well as pupils – this should not be underestimated, as the Prescribed Drama activity can be dependent on the leaders creating and sustaining the appropriate play responses.

• **Rules** – maybe with the idea of some fictional sanction in a safe situation.

• **An element of tension or atmosphere:** turn-taking, repetitive, involving feelings of anticipation of some peak of excitement or disaster, and elements of fear or threat in a 'safe' situation.

• **A ritual element,** maybe controlled by music, a rhythm or a rhyme, to reinforce commitment to the activity.

• **Communal activity,** involving all staff and pupils, with minimal extraneous distractions as far as possible – as indicated above, the 'shared emotional experience' can be crucially dependent on the leaders generating the appropriate play responses.

• **Elements of cross-curricular learning,** or ways of motivating learning; for example:

> *PE* – movement, stability, fine touch;
>
> *Science* – discovering materials (sensory experiences); self-awareness; cause-effect;
>
> *Mathematics* – shape and space concepts, number, prediction, problem solving;
>
> *English* – communication: vocalization, signing, eye-pointing, speaking, listening, participating verbally in a group, responding appropriately to instructions, literacy;
>
> *PSE* – practising life-skills (personal independence); membership of a group, relating to others – behaviour, interaction, cooperation, shared emotions; developing attention, concentration, choices, decision making;
>
> *History* – sequencing events;
>
> *Music* – group singing and playing, controlling sounds – dynamics, tempo;
>
> *Technology* – identifying a need; expressing ideas to meet a need;
>
> *Geography* – following directions, human occupations, environments;
>
> *Art* – representing something observed, imagined and remembered in visual form.

Props

Teacher or assistant in role as bus driver (denoted by peaked hat); tickets; real or pretend money; portable felt-board to represent 'window' on bus with individual pictures/photos of typical things in the countryside that make sounds (tractor, cow, etc.) – one picture per child; cassette and sound tape to correspond with pictures.

Preparation

Arrange chairs in the room to represent a bus. Put teacher or assistant into role in front of group – children to help install 'bus driver' with tickets. Pupils to form queue for the bus (standing or sitting may be easier!).

Implementation

Tell group that we're going on a bus into the countryside: 'I wonder what we'll see'. First child to board bus, whilst everyone chants or sings (to the tune of 'The Wheels on the Bus'):

> *[Susan's] going for a ride*
> *On a bus to the countryside.*
> *She buys her ticket, sits inside,*
> *What do you think she heard and spied?*

Having obtained a ticket, the seated child looks through the bus window represented by the felt-board with pictures. The sound tape plays the first sound for the child to identify. Pictures may be removed and placed on communication boards on wheelchairs or replaced with Bliss or Makaton symbols to enable physically disabled pupils to eye-point from a more restricted selection. The next pupil then boards the bus . . . and so on, each in turn.

Suggestions

Level 1 – limited response: pupils may be led or wheeled onto the bus and buy their tickets with help; instead of identifying sounds individually, play sound tape and project corresponding images onto large screen (black-out for greater atmosphere and to sharpen senses) – do pupils turn to locate source of sound? Do they look at the images?

Level 2 – active response, not necessarily verbal: run activity as described above.

Level 3 – interactive response (verbal or signing): run activity as described above; in addition, pupil to purchase ticket from bus driver with appropriate social graces (and money skills?)

Open-ended – unexpected outcome for pupils to resolve: run activity as described, but inject a problem. Example: explain to group that we are going to visit Aunt Lucy; on the way the bus breaks down (driver briefed ahead of session). Reactions? Baldly practical solution – repair the bus ('Have you seen the size of that wheel? Slowly now, altogether, one, two, three, lift . . .'). Or more realistic – how can we let Aunt Lucy know, she'll be worried? (Make a phone call – public phone? Ask at farmhouse?). Group could practise skills before trying them out 'for real' in the drama (drama within the drama!). Follow the group's initiatives as far as possible, but slow them down to think through the situation, and lead them to discover the implications of their actions and decisions.

Drama convention – stimulus for or contextualized strategy in open-ended drama.

NB Adapt activity for a different transport and/or sights and sounds, eg: train, city, etc.

Using Prescribed Drama Structures

When playing Prescribed Drama activities, it is important that they are experienced in a fun, relaxed atmosphere, in order to generate the appropriate 'play' responses. Chances of this will be increased by the teacher thoroughly familiarizing him or herself with the activity beforehand, and having all the necessary props readily to hand, with assistant staff thoroughly briefed. The teacher needs to be flexible and be prepared to adapt the activities to suit the particular group – experiment without the song or rhyme perhaps. He or she also needs to be sensitive to the concentration span of the particular group – some may play for an hour or more, whilst for others, a short 10–15 minute session would suffice.

Prescribed Drama events can provide a further enriching experience for pupils, by linking together a series of individual Prescribed Drama Structures based on a theme so that they are experienced in succession. They can involve some organizing and both time and space in setting-up, but can be well worth the effort. Some drama events packs are commercially available, for example 'Funfair' and 'Galaxies' from the LDA. They aim to provide multi-sensory experiences through the drama, and come complete with audio-tape of music and story-line, and clear instructions on preparing for and implementing the activities. There need be no reason, however, why practitioners may not devise their own Prescribed Drama event, by linking a series of Prescribed Drama Structures in succession on a theme, tailor-made to the needs of their particular pupils, and perhaps on a topic currently being developed in the school concerned.

Level 1 – limited engagement

Activities at this level rely on surprise elements and sudden changes in pace or atmosphere. Staff will need to work as a team and define clearly the changes in mood, in order to communicate what is significant to the group and to create the shared experience. Activities at this level need not require any movement on the part of the group – participation need only be passive or receptive, although the teacher may find ways to pitch them for those more physically able pupils. The teacher would begin to look for albeit limited response – laughter, smiles, spontaneous vocalization, a sense of anticipation . . . an awareness of a change in mood and atmosphere.

Level 2 – active response

Activities at this level will be appropriate for those pupils able to pick up rules of procedure, even if verbal comprehension and expression may be limited. The activities require the pupils to make a physical response or active contribution, although not necessarily verbal. There are opportunities for verbal involvement, however (such as joining in the songs), and the teacher should also be prepared to absorb and indeed encourage spontaneous verbal interaction in the make-believe (such as with a teacher in role). Activities at this level also include an element of problem solving: physical control, a conceptual task maybe . . . as far as possible, participants should be allowed to resolve these themselves, so fostering a sense of initiative and resourcefulness.

Level 3 – interactive response

Activities at this level require a verbal or signing response by the participants and tend to be conceptually more demanding. The teacher will be able to find ways to adapt them however, to meet the needs of less able pupils – all pupils should have their turn, whatever their ability, in order to foster the notion that drama will only work if everyone 'plays the game' (drama is a group activity, based on shared experiences). Similarly, all participants should be encouraged to make the appropriate responses, adapting their behaviour in the light of the make-believe, even if they need help to do so.

Open-ended Prescribed Drama

Here, the 'lid is taken off' the expected outcome of the activity, so that the pupils are on their mettle to resolve a situation. Very often the teacher may be able to anticipate certain responses; however, he or she should be open-minded, and seek to lead the pupils to discover the implications of their suggestions and work towards a satisfactory outcome. It may be possible to pitch responses at different levels of ability – accepting a baldly practical contribution from one pupil, but demanding considerable negotiation skills from another.

At this point, open-ended Prescribed Drama activities closely resemble open-ended drama proper – and so they should, because really they can act as a bridge into planning and structuring make-believe for learning, taking play into drama. I feel it is helpful at this stage, however, for teacher and pupils together just to begin to 'get the feel' of negotiating within the make-believe, and to build up confidence in handling and structuring choices and decisions 'on the hoof'. By opening up a Prescribed Drama Structure, the teacher is essentially 'opening up a game'. Even though it has become more open, the whole thing still hinges on that original 'game', so the teacher is able to retain a clear grip on what to do within a secure structure. It is really the same process as planning in open-ended drama proper (see Chapter 4), and in fact, the kind of activity could be described equally as adhering to a tightly-planned lesson model. However, from the teacher's point of view, by thinking of it as an open-ended Prescribed Drama activity, both he or she and the pupils are able to gain familiarity with the drama form without yet worrying over the mechanics of planning and exploring the range of options for structuring drama.

Progressing in Understanding Drama

There are no hard and fast rules as to:

- who may play which drama activity on what particular level, and
- at what point it becomes appropriate to move on to a new activity or a new level.

This will depend on:

- the teacher's confidence in taking risks and handling increasingly open-ended situations;
- the teacher's perception of the needs of the group to face a new challenge.

Progress with a group within Prescribed Drama Structures may happen in different ways over varying time scales according to the needs of both the teacher and the group. Activities bear repeating time and again: as the pupils become familiar with the Prescribed Drama Structure, so their confidence and readiness to engage in make-believe will develop. Some groups may take weeks, terms or years to progress to a new level with a more demanding challenge. With others it may be possible to progress quickly and take them in to more open-ended work within a session or two. Progress may be achieved by:

• adapting the same Prescribed Drama Structure to present a new challenge;
• proceeding to a different Prescribed Drama Structure at the same level (horizontal progress);
• proceeding to a new Prescribed Drama at a higher level;
• proceeding to an open-ended Prescribed Drama.

In this way, both teacher and group are all gradually eased into more open-ended drama work. The 'Bus Ride' Prescribed Drama Structure illustrates how progress may be achieved *within* the same activity, by pitching the demands and engagement within the make-believe from the pupils accordingly. Nevertheless, there may well come a point where many of the pupils are ready for a new challenge, the teacher feels reasonably confident he or she can handle it, but there are certain pupils who are still developmentally discovering make-believe and the essence of drama activity. Things become rather more complicated. What then?

One option may be to 'stream' drama, combining pupils from different teaching groups according to their level. Alternatively, my preferred approach is to retain the original class group, in the belief that drama can consider what people have in common: universal themes and issues. I then endeavour to ensure that at some point in an open-ended drama, I include a Prescribed Drama Structure, but *contextualized* within the drama. Rather than standing as an activity complete in itself (which of course it could), it then becomes part of the unfolding make-believe on the way to the resolution of a particular problem or situation or possibly even as a stimulus for the drama. In this way, less able pupils may be reached, and enabled to progress with an activity pitched at their appropriate level, whilst nevertheless experiencing the 'group buzz' and acquiring the 'sense of play' as part of the wider developing drama. Those more able pupils will also benefit: group identity is reaffirmed and pupils have a chance to refocus, kept 'on task'; the drama may be usefully slowed down at this point, so preventing the pupils from rushing on superficially. This is illustrated in 'Farmer Bailey', an example of an open-ended drama lesson in Chapter 4.

To summarize

Whilst necessarily limiting in a drama sense, because it tends to preclude innovation by the pupils and because it does not really challenge their make-believe, a Prescribed Drama Structure can have several valuable uses and applications, and can be used flexibly:

- **For developing** the necessary elements of make-believe for drama:
  - a sense of play – an emerging awareness of make-believe, however limited;
  - commitment – the idea that it will only work if everyone will 'suspend disbelief';
  - accepting roles and symbols;
  - reacting to and adapting their own behaviour in the light of the make-believe.

- **For establishing** group cohesion, enabling a new teacher/group to get to know each other within a secure structured drama framework, so developing confidence for working together in drama.
- **For assessing** readily where individual pupils are in terms of their development in drama (eg, do they accept the teacher in role? Are they able to make contact with others within the make-believe? Are they able to maintain commitment to the fictitious context? etc.).
- **For adapting** to allow for increasing innovation and response by individual pupils within the make-believe: relatively passive – active but not necessarily verbal – interactive (verbal or signing).
- **For challenging** the pupils by suddenly putting them on their mettle, having to resolve an unexpected outcome.
- **For contextualizing** as part of an open-ended drama lesson, ie, as a drama convention, another strategy in the drama teacher's repertoire of ways to organize the drama.
- **For extending language:** activities work well not just in the first language, but also a second language – I have devised several versions in French, for example.

There are further examples of Prescribed Drama activities at different levels of engagement within the make-believe in the Appendix. I have made suggestions for developing the activities. I have indicated how I have used the activities for different purposes with pupils with differing special educational needs, and also, in some cases, how I have used and/or adapted the same activity by turning the tables on the expected with very different outcomes (open-ended Prescribed Drama). In this way, the participants are enabled to begin to play freely and spontaneously in the make-believe. Once they have achieved this, they are ready to have their play challenged and to use drama as a medium for learning.

CHAPTER 4

'Drama Fluency' – towards using drama as a learning medium

This chapter will look at the mechanics of the drama process: planning and structuring open-ended drama for use as a medium for learning ('drama fluency'). It will look at ways to challenge the pupils' make-believe play and take it into open-ended drama to explore a learning area. The teacher will make judgements about the learning area to be explored based on the needs of the pupils and what may be preferable with regards to the content and suitability of the material and its potential for exploration and learning through the drama. The range of options available to the teacher for structuring open-ended drama (the drama teacher's 'tool kit') will be considered more fully in the next chapter.

A Model for the Drama Process

The model below represents the underlying process of all drama lessons where the pupils' make-believe play is challenged and learning areas explored. Essentially four stages are worked through:

> *identifying a topic – getting it going – deepening belief – exploring a learning area*

On establishing the topic for the drama, the teacher involves the pupils in creating and setting up the make-believe and works to deepen their belief and commitment in a commonly agreed fiction. He or she then watches for a point where they appear to be taking advantage of the make-believe, in order to 'suspend the plot' by putting the brakes on and then making them work at resolving the situation.

The point of this is to explore potential areas of learning as revealed by the pupils' ideas, attitudes and preconceptions, by considering the implications of their suggestions and behaviour. The drama is therefore on two levels: 'the play for the pupils' and the 'play for the teacher' (Geoff Gilham, 1974). To refer again to John Taylor's (1986a) vivid metaphor of Frankenstein's Monster, of a created thing that somehow turns on itself:

> In any drama lesson the teacher is looking to arrive at one or more key moments in which there is a transfer from the phase of creating the drama world to the phase of coping with the implications of the world created. . . . Moments when the Monster awakes. (p.19)

21

Entering the Drama

- _Stage 1:_ SELECTING THE TOPIC
  - teacher/pupil idea?
  - stimulus for the drama? (a picture? object? letter? a story?)
  - what's in it for them?
  - what's in it for me? Is an obvious learning area already apparent?

- _Stage 2:_ INITIATION PHASE (_getting the drama going!_)
  - Roles   – who are the pupils?
    - who am I?
  - Place   – where are we?
  - Focus   – what are we doing?
    - opening attitude? (how do we feel about this?)

- _Stage 3:_ DIAGNOSTIC PHASE (_creating the make-believe_)
  - work to deepen belief in the drama (variable number of strategies)
  - present 'problem'. . . how does the group respond?
  - be on the look-out for possible learning areas that may arise
  - teacher makes decision as to the group's learning need
  - teacher may have anticipated certain lines of development, but should remain flexible

- _Stage 4:_ INTERVENTION PHASE (_confronting the make-believe_)
  - work to challenge/resolve situation (variable number of strategies)
  - exploring a learning area
  - use of dramatic tension to make meaning

Selecting the topic

The pupils may suggest an idea for the drama and the teacher asks him or herself, 'What's in it for the pupils – what is it about this particular theme that is so appealing?' and then 'What's in it for me – how can I begin to challenge their perception in some way?' It is often the case that pupils with special educational needs become obsessed with a particular theme, and because they may lack the mental agility of their mainstream peers, they may not be able to see the appeal or inherent interest of an alternative idea or suggestion. If they are not going to 'switch off' altogether, the drama teacher may be stuck in having to work on a particular theme, such as a popular television series. For example, I was once involved in such a situation, based on the TV programme _The A Team._ I asked myself what it was that appealed to the pupils. Was it the glory and glamour of a secret fighting force . . . but what if the A Team makes a mistake such as blowing up the wrong car? What would be the consequences of this and how would they be answerable for their mistake?

It may be that the pupils' imagination is captivated by a familiar story, such as _Little Red Riding Hood._ The teacher would begin to ask him or herself why this should be – excitement of wandering where there might be impending danger perhaps? The teacher would then seek to lead the group to consider the implications of this behaviour, and to explore the learning area; in this case, appropriate behaviour if you fancy going for a walk in the woods (Tell someone where you are going first? Do not go into woods alone? etc.). This would not be achieved by straightforward 'acting out the story', although admittedly, this would be fun in itself and certainly help bring the story to life. It would not constitute drama however, because no preconceptions would be challenged, the pupils being preoccupied more with the unfolding story-line, and the teacher perhaps more concerned with how well the parts were being acted. What if the drama instead concerned itself with a scene not in the conventional story-line, but no less relevant: Red Riding Hood's parent (teacher), rushing frantically round the village on the edge of the woods, asking everyone (pupils) if they've seen Red Riding Hood because she is very late home – could they help? (Join in a search party? – discovering on a feeling level the real dangers of the 'adventure' but in the safety of being one step removed; or alternatively, giving advice to the parent on what to say to Red Riding Hood to prevent it happening again?).

Sometimes a learning area within a topic may be apparent from the outset, as in the previous examples. Sometimes the teacher may have in mind a teaching-point he or she wants to confront, such as 'taking responsibility for something entrusted to your care', and would then look to contrive a scenario or dramatic context in which this could be explored. However, a learning area may only become evident as the make-believe unfolds. The actual topic might seem vague (eg, the seaside), so the teacher would aim to get the drama going and be on the look-out for the pupils' interests becoming apparent as the drama unfolds. The teacher would adopt a similar approach if a stimulus is to provide the starting-point for drama (picture, photograph, an object, a piece of music, etc.).

Initiation phase

The teacher looks to get the drama going by establishing who everybody is (roles), exactly where they are (eg, if at the seaside, are they on the prom, the pier or the beach? It may be necessary to narrow the focus quite considerably to give pupils a clear and plausible motivation), and exactly what they are doing (again, to narrow the focus), and how they feel (pleased to be on holiday? Sad because it's the last day and they have to leave?). The drama at the outset could be fixed by any one of these in any order, as long as all aspects are established. With some groups, it may take a while to set up the drama, constantly cross-checking to make sure everyone is 'with' it. With other groups, they may enter instantly into the make-believe with only one of the elements established at the outset. Alternatively, the pupils may negotiate all elements from the outset.

Diagnostic phase

The teacher then works through a variable number of drama conventions – different ways of organizing the drama – to create the make-believe and deepen the participants' commitment and belief in the make-believe. He or she will be watching what the pupils do, and looking to diagnose a 'learning need'. There will come a point where the participants appear to be taking advantage of the fiction, or maybe reveal an attitude which the teacher feels compelled to explore (eg, 'There are so many nice people in this wood, aren't there?'. In this example, the teacher would perhaps want to expose the pupils to a situation in the make-believe where they have to deal with 'Stranger Danger', and work at resolving this situation successfully.)

Maybe no such learning area is yet apparent, in which case perhaps the teacher might contrive a problem and look to introduce it suddenly or gradually. Alternatively, maybe the teacher has anticipated introducing a particular problem, and even possible lines of development according to how the pupils react and respond. The important thing is for the teacher to remain flexible, and be on the look-out for possible learning-areas that may arise, and to be prepared to abandon an original plan if necessary.

Intervention phase

Finally, the teacher intervenes to confront implications revealed in the drama, and to make the group work to resolve the situation. He or she achieves this through the selective application of a variable number of drama conventions and the use of elements of the drama form, in particular dramatic tension. With experience, the teacher senses how long to sustain the drama in order for the learning area to be explored – it may be a sudden or gradual realization for the pupils, to be reflected on and discussed more fully out of role perhaps.

Understanding and Using Drama for Learning

The 'Farmer Bailey' open-ended drama lesson is designed for a mixed-ability group of MLD/SLD pupils, possibly with PMLD youngsters integrated. Within the plan, I have contextualized the 'Bus Ride' Prescribed Drama Structure (see Chapter 3). Whilst the Prescribed Drama Structure can be enjoyed at all levels of ability, and pitched according to the participants' ability to engage within the make-believe, it is serving to deepen belief in the drama, so preventing the pupils from rushing superficially headlong. It is also serving to enable the less able youngsters to *learn how to do drama whilst doing it,* by teaching them the elements of make-believe play.

This interrelationship between the content of a drama (what it is about and what we can learn from it) and the drama form itself (how the learning is achieved) is present in drama and theatre work at all levels of sophistication. It is important that both aspects are continually developed in pupils:

- that they become increasingly proficient in engaging in the drama process, using the medium to explore areas of learning;
- that they understand how particular ways of organizing the drama enable aspects of learning to be shared and communicated.

Example: ***FARMER BAILEY***   **OPEN-ENDED DRAMA**

stimulus
drama game

> *TOPIC (establishing theme for the drama)*
> Present Farmer Bailey's hat - pass it round as all chant:
>
> > *Farmer Bailey's here today*
> > *Farmer Bailey will not play*
> > *What does Farmer Bailey say?*
> > (person with hat puts it on and says angrily:)
> > *Leave me alone and go away!*
>
> Tell group Farmer Bailey lives in the country – I hope we
> don't meet him, because we're going on a picnic.

preparation for
teacher in role

use of space

ritual

use of space

> *INITIATION PHASE (getting it going)*
> Create countryside following group's suggestions, using
> masking tape to demarcate (tree, river, FB's house, etc.).
> Show empty picnic box – each child to think of food item and
> put it in box (prompt with real items or pictures if necessary).
> Arrange chairs at one end of room to represent bus. Pupils to
> sit in queue at the 'bus stop' waiting.

Prescribed
Drama
Structure

movement

structured play

improvisation

teacher in role

> *DIAGNOSTIC PHASE (deepen belief - assess learning need)*
> Run 'Bus Ride' activity, adjusting to relative ability levels of
> pupils – see 'Bus Ride' Prescribed Drama Structure.
> Arrival in countryside. Use bench or upturned chair to
> represent a stile. Two supporting adults to lift each child in
> turn as high as possible over stile (older pupils could assist
> each other). Physically disabled pupils could be swung over
> stile in the picnic blanket.
> Group to sit in 'field' near Farmer Bailey's house to have
> picnic. (Reactions? Be on look-out for possible learning area).
> Produce real item of food to share out (eg, packet of biscuits).
> Make excuse to leave, having obtained assurance that they
> will be sensible and look after the picnic (supporting staff to
> remain with group if available).
>
> (Decide learning need. Group to resolve possible problem and
> explore learning area presented by – range of options)

Possible crisis? eg, snake bite, injury, bull on loose (practical problem)	Tramp appears –would they give up their food? (moral dilemma)	Attractive stranger attempts to offer sweets for their picnic? (saying No!)	Farmer Bailey appears, angry at their behaviour (Country Code)

INTERVENTION PHASE

(lead group to resolve one of these avenues through a succession of strategies)

25

a) *TIGHTLY-PLANNED LESSON*

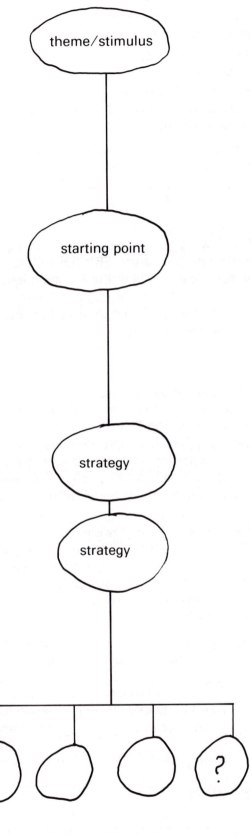

Topic

– selected by teacher, or supplied by pupils beforehand

Initiation phase:

– opening action planned by teacher (roles, place, focus and attitude)

Diagnostic phase:

– number of conventions variable

– teacher on the look-out for pupil interests and other possible learning areas that may arise, and prepared to abandon original plan.

Intervention phase:

– teacher may have in mind several possible outcomes, but should be flexible

b) PARTIALLY-PLANNED LESSON

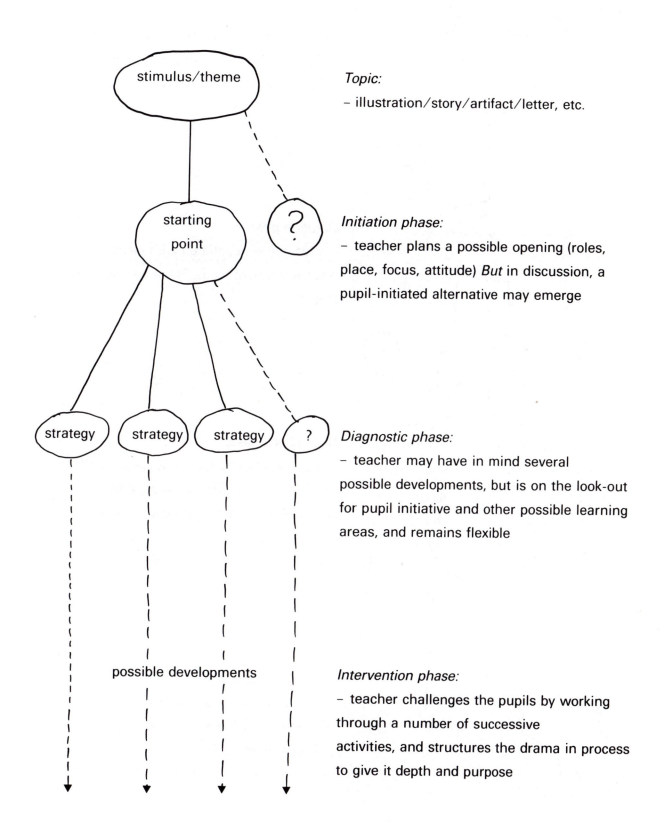

Topic:
– illustration/story/artifact/letter, etc.

Initiation phase:
– teacher plans a possible opening (roles, place, focus, attitude) *But* in discussion, a pupil-initiated alternative may emerge

Diagnostic phase:
– teacher may have in mind several possible developments, but is on the look-out for pupil initiative and other possible learning areas, and remains flexible

Intervention phase:
– teacher challenges the pupils by working through a number of successive activities, and structures the drama in process to give it depth and purpose

c) *OPEN LESSON*

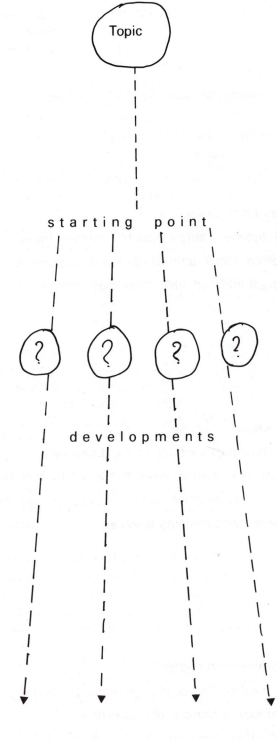

Topic

– class gather round 'discussion chair'

. . . suggestions for drama on board,

. . . vote taken, consensus gained

starting point

Initiation phase:

– roles/place negotiated with class;

teacher provides focus/issue and opening

attitude

developments

Diagnostic phase:

– teacher watches for the way the pupils

seem to want the drama to go, and

diagnoses their learning need

Intervention phase:

– teacher uses a number of

drama conventions to make pupils work at

achieving goals

28

Drama Lesson Models

Whilst the deep structure or process of all drama lessons is the same, the surface structure will vary tremendously, according to how the teacher chooses to organize a lesson to enable the pupils to engage with the content of the drama. The drama teacher will call on a range of drama conventions and elements of the drama form to make meaning (see Chapter 5). The extent to which these are preplanned by the drama teacher will dictate the kind of lesson model chosen.

The following models illustrate possible ways to structure the drama according to the extent of the planning ahead of the session. The Appendix contains actual examples of these models in practice, with the meat on the bones. There are three models:

- **tightly-planned** – the component activities are anticipated with planned elements of freedom, with a possible learning area already in mind;
- **partially-planned** – a way into the drama already anticipated, along with additional strategies to deepen belief, and several directions for the drama anticipated, although a learning area is not necessarily yet apparent;
- **open** – all decisions and choices concerning the direction of the drama to be negotiated from the outset.

Working in Role

This section is perhaps misplaced, coming at the *end* of this chapter. However, it is offered by way of a postscript to the explanation of the mechanics of planning for drama and as a lead into the next chapter which covers options available for adding flesh to the skeleton. Implicit, and indeed central to the developmental approach proposed in *Drama For All*, is development of proficiency in working in role – in the teacher just as much as in the pupils. Drama should be about negotiated learning between the participants, with the teacher giving it shape, depth and purpose in process. The teacher represents one half of the bargaining process, therefore he or she needs ultimately to develop the same skills as the pupils of selecting focus, injecting tension and creating meaningful symbols (Gavin Bolton, 1979).

The most immediate and direct way of achieving this is through working in role. It is easily the most effective strategy with pupils with special educational needs, as it enables the teacher to negotiate with the pupils within the make-believe, without having to break the tension of the developing fiction, or confusing the pupils by demanding that they themselves nip in and out of role in order to consider the direction of the drama. It also avoids complex language constructions: instead of having to use language for prediction or recall (eg, 'What would you do if. . .?'), language can remain in the here-and-now, through talking to the participants directly in role. Techniques and ways of working in role will be discussed more fully in Chapter 5; Chapter 6 also deals with certain difficulties sometimes encountered by the teacher when working in role.

Working in role can seem a huge psychological hurdle, but one that is actually quickly and easily overcome (honest!). I broke it by talking as Snow White (wearing a red hairband) for ten minutes to a lively group of junior-age pupils with severe learning difficulties: Snow White was very fed up and lonely, stuck doing the housework for the dwarves all day. . . could they think of a way to cheer me up? (They decided to give me a present, and I asked each in turn to offer me something appropriate, with which I professed delight.) Think of 'role' simply as a 'mantle' – talking to the pupils *as if* you were someone else, not going for an Oscar-winning performance! Teachers and assistants very often have little problem joining in pupils' spontaneous make-believe in the playground or home-corner, or in dramatized story-telling; it is merely a structured version of the same thing. Besides, teachers 'act'/adopt a persona/role-play the minute they step in front of a class. It is a case of the teacher consciously harnessing the same skills and using the same kind of signals, but speaking as another character.

Hopefully, using the approach proposed in this chapter, where working in role is integral to the framework, will enable the teacher to get used to handling and manipulating pupils' responses. Initially this may be in the security of a predictable structure, which may then become more open-ended as the teacher's confidence develops in relinquishing control and responsibility for the direction of the drama to the pupils. Crucial will be the development of the teacher's ability to spot learning areas as they arise, and to give the evolving drama structure and purpose in process by drawing on a range of possible strategies and conventions. The quality of a learning experience in classroom drama can only be as good as the teacher enables it to be. This puts a considerable onus on the teacher to develop his or her practice and range of options on ways to organize the drama. It is time to open the 'Tool Kit'.

CHAPTER 5

The Drama Teacher's Tool Kit – drama conventions and strategies

Once pupils have become 'drama literate' and have grasped the essential elements of make-believe play necessary for drama in and through Prescribed Drama activities, they will be ready to become 'drama fluent' – to have their make-believe play challenged and confronted, to use drama as a learning medium. In order to achieve this, the teacher will need to structure the drama to create learning opportunities. The previous chapter described the principles of the *drama process,* how content (a topic or theme) could be explored to achieve greater understanding and insight by the participants. This chapter will look at the kinds of options available for structuring the drama, to enable meanings to be generated through the interrelationship arising from the selective application of:

- **elements of the drama form** to give depth and quality of experience, to create and build on tensions implicit in the material, which will give a sense of urgency and momentum for the drama – its 'imperative tension' (Gavin Bolton, 1992);
- **drama conventions** – different ways to organize the drama, to enable the participants to engage with the content and face the challenges presented by this 'imperative tension';
- **teaching strategies** – additional options for organizing the drama that are also common to other teaching contexts.

Somehow, it is as if anyone ought to be able to 'do drama', but no one would have the same expectations from a maths lesson. Yet it is the same in drama: there are certain conventions that are simply beyond pupils just venturing into 'drama literacy', ie, just beginning to grasp the elements of make-believe play necessary for drama. Learning in drama will take place when pupils experience the relationship between the *content* of the drama and the drama *form*, and make connections between the make-believe situation and the real world. It is thus crucial that the teacher structures the drama by selecting conventions appropriate to the ability of the pupils, drawing on suitable elements of the drama form that will be accessible to the participants, to enable them to explore tensions inherent in the material (the content). It is through this interrelationship of content, form and process that participants will *make meaning*, and so be able to use drama as a learning medium. However, as Gavin Bolton (1992, p.116) points out:

A participant's focus of attention is primarily on creating an art product (through illustrative/performance activity) or creating a fictitious social context (through dramatic playing). Learning occurs at a level of, to use Polanyi's (1958) useful term, 'subsidiary awareness'.

In pupils with special educational needs in particular, one cannot assume that connections have been made and that learning has taken place. It is crucially important therefore, that the teacher does his or her best to structure the drama to enable maximum *engagement* by the participants in the dramatic activity. In addition, as Gavin Bolton (1992, p.117) reminds us, *detachment* from the dramatic activity will be equally important:

It is a double featured process:

- detaching oneself from the content in order to examine it and learn from it;
- detaching oneself from the theatre form in order to examine how something was achieved.

There are many excellent publications that deal in depth with ways to structure classroom drama. Here therefore, I shall give merely a brief explanation of those that I use regularly, and indicate their appropriateness and usefulness for pupils with special educational needs.

The Drama Form

As stated above, the teacher will need to draw on elements of the drama form to create the momentum for the drama, a reason for the participants to care and feel impelled into action. Jonothan Neelands (1990) comprehensively encapsulates facets of the drama form. I shall summarize these briefly here, and indicate how they may be used to enhance meaning for pupils with special educational needs.

Language

- Communication and interaction between the participants, in and out of role;
- symbolic use of language to represent a situation or character's speech;
- non-verbal language through the use of movement, symbol and visual imagery.

The drama teacher needs to ensure that the level of language is pitched according to the ability of those pupils with special educational needs, with communication supported with signing systems as necessary. If the pupils are to be enabled to make meanings, then this has to be accessed at their respective level of conceptual development. For those unable yet to relate solely to the spoken word, communication will have to be supported with real objects, toys or miniature objects, photos or picture material, according to the individual's level of symbolic understanding. Drama can be instrumental in promoting language skills and appropriate use of language in context (as indicated in Chapter 1).

Relationships of time

- The notion of 'elastic time', where the drama may unfold at life-rate, or may be stopped, accelerated and replayed;
- the actuality of the drama happening in the here-and-now, and being unreplicable.

Many pupils with special educational needs find concepts of time problematic: chopping about and jumping between past, present and future may be very confusing, and would need to be very clearly defined. For example, with some groups it may be possible to clarify moments in time captured in the drama, by scenes taking place in different parts of the drama space, or having a demarcated space (possibly enhanced by use of lighting) to indicate a flashback. The use of 'action replay' may also be helpful for revising or re-examining a scene that has just taken place. With other groups, however, it is preferable to stick with a 'living through' drama that takes place in the here-and-now. Recording the lesson on video may allow the drama to be considered in a narrative sense, as a story that happened in the past. This may then contribute to the students' learning about the concertina use of the convention of time in drama, particularly if the previous lesson is then developed in a subsequent one and so becomes a 'rolling drama'. Even students with severe learning difficulties will often recognize and relate to this genre through familiarity with 'soap operas' on TV!

Relationships of space

- Symbolic use of space to convey meanings, eg, status between characters, physical surroundings and psychological distance in relationships.
- the expectation from the 'acting space' or set as a place where meanings will be created;
- the discovery of the potential of the space during improvisation to enhance meaning and build belief.

This element of the drama form can be critical in enhancing meaning for students with special needs, by providing visual 'hooks' with which they can engage. The drama teacher should maximize opportunities to help the students into the symbolism through adapting the environment and involving them in creating the 'set' for the drama. Whilst the creation of an elaborate 'environment' may help the participants into the make-believe, the complete opposite can also be valuable – starting with a blank set and using pupil ideas and initiatives to block out areas.

Social interaction

Drama depends on creative interaction between participants:

- on the real dimension (discussing, planning, organizing, reviewing);
- on the symbolic level (interacting within a convention which temporarily supersedes the real dimension).

The social skills required cannot be assumed when dealing in drama with pupils with special educational needs. It is possible to work on the 'social health' of the group from within the drama (eg, elevating the status of a particular student by acting on his or her initiative), and through using conventions that intrinsically demand cooperation and negotiation (eg, Prescribed Drama Structures, movement, ritual, drama game, physical task, etc.). Nevertheless, to a greater or lesser degree, many students with special educational needs will struggle to generate and sustain interaction within the make-believe. The upshot is that the teacher may not have available the full range of options with regard to group work, and he or she should not assume that the participants will be able to take over 'ownership' of the drama as readily as many of their mainstream peers.

Dramatic tension

Dramatic tension has to be the key to creating quality of experience and something that the drama teacher has to learn to sense, control and manipulate. In a useful article that appeared in *London Drama* magazine (1982, p.16), students on the advanced drama diploma course at Durham University invite the reader to consider. . .

> Has this ever happened to you? That well prepared forty minute lesson that was over in two minutes! The children stormed the castle – knocked over the giant – and stole the treasure! WHAT WENT WRONG? What was missing?

The answer is *dramatic tension*. They continue the article by illustrating some of the ways meaning could have been added to the above example, to prevent the children mindlessly storming the castle, by adding dramatic tension.

> EXAMPLE:
> 1) *'Someone may be watching and listening - take care!'* eg, the giant – the trees – the stone faces on the castle walls.
> 2) *'How can we get in?'* – (planning our entry) – getting past the guard – or – tricking the giant to open the door – or – solving the puzzle that opens the door – or– making our disguise.
> 3) *'Have you thought how big everything will be?'* – (the relative size of giant land) eg – The grass is tall – the insects huge – the mice are monstrous – the walls are high, the gates heavy – the size of the key.
> 4) *Planning and practising our strategies* – eg – what danger signals shall we use? – who will act as look out? – let's practise them!
> 5) *Instructing the inept and frightened teacher in role.* . . .

The above example illustrates very clearly the way the teacher can spot tensions inherent in the material, moments of good 'theatre' almost, and can use it to put the brakes on, to slow the drama down and make the participants confront the make-believe situation that has been created. Tensions may not be fully apparent at first, but with practice the teacher can learn to rely on his or her ability to recognize them as the drama unfolds, and to sense just how long to sustain it without the children switching off and losing interest.

The teacher will be able to enhance the pupils' experience in drama through sensitive handling of the following.

• **Appropriate atmosphere** – to help give belief to the dramatic context and in enabling the pupils to identify with the action on a feeling level. For pupils with special educational needs, this may be critical in enabling them to engage in make-believe, to sense and relate to something 'other' than their usual frame of reference. This may be achieved in the make-believe through:

– *the use of physical devices* (eg, lighting, special effects, costume, etc.);
– *certain drama conventions* which by their very nature intrinsically generate tension (eg, teacher-in-role, ritual, action replay — see the next section 'Drama Conventions');
– *supporting staff* generating or 'modelling' appropriate responses.

• **Appropriate rhythm and pace** – to enable the pupils to gain the sense of objectivity to learn in and through the drama medium – doing drama with the awareness of doing it at the same time. With pupils with special educational needs, especially where there may be an extreme range of ability within a group, rhythm and pace will have to be finely tuned in order to sustain and generate tension and a sense of urgency in all the participants. The teacher will need to:
– *move at a pace suitable for the group;* for example, PMLD pupils may be thrown into spasm through too sudden a change – 'shocks' as such must be used very selectively; a highly volatile group may need thoughtful static strategies, initially at least, to keep them 'on task' and to establish a collective consensus and focus for the drama; a more withdrawn group may benefit from a sudden acceleration in pace to prompt them into a response;
– *allow time and opportunity for reflection,* both within the drama and afterwards out of role (crucial in enabling pupils to transfer and generalize learning from the drama to the real world);
– *allow for an ebb and flow of action,* with the use of a variety of drama conventions, to help focus attention and enable pupils with limited concentration spans to 'come and go';
– *balance active and passive engagement,* (participant/percipient within the drama) with individual and group involvement, particularly with consideration for certain pupils with physical and sensory disabilities who literally may not be able to sustain the pace;
– *operate within physical limitations,* with awareness and sensitivity to extraneous factors such as space available, noise thresholds, timetabling demands – failure to acknowledge institutional constraints can have disastrous consequences in a special school situation where the school day is already shortened and pressures on the timetable are considerable, with pupils 'bussed' often over a considerable radius.

When working with pupils with special educational needs, the teacher will have to find ways to make sure that tension is experienced by everyone, through signals that are very blatant, clear and uncomplicated –

subtlety may well be totally missed. He or she may even have to find ways of repeating or rephrasing a point several times, to ensure that everyone is 'with' the drama before it proceeds further, and to give slower pupils a chance to 'catch up' with the action. The above-mentioned article provides a useful summary of different tension structures. Similarly, several notable drama books also deal in some detail with dramatic tension (for example, Gavin Bolton, 1979; Cecily O'Neill and Alan Lambert, 1982). I will indicate here certain ways of introducing tension that I have found successful with groups of pupils with special educational needs and refer to actual lessons outlined in the Appendix.

Tension of time
• *Delaying* – new recruits to hospital staff itching to get to work on the ward are made to go through irritating suitability tests ('Teamwork').
• *Anticipation of an event* – pandemonium resulting from 'near miss' when kerb drill not carried out correctly ('Crossing the Road').
• *Urgency* – Aunty Glad/Cinderella tired and fed up at having to do all the housework themselves – can anyone please help? (before Ugly Sisters return?) ('Aunty Glad').

Tension of situation
• *Secrecy* – would everyone keep their promise not to tell the Ugly Sister that they had helped Cinderella? ('Aunty Glad').
• *Mystery* – why isn't Roberta in her garden or answering the door? ('No Answer').
• *Confrontation* – tension from a fraught relationship, as picnickers are confronted by angry farmer ('Country Code').
• *Blocking* – attempts at peaceful protest against proposed development of woodland conservation area are thwarted, when wealthy new land-owner announces she is proceeding regardless ('Theme Park').
• *Dilemma* – conflicting loyalties to friend who has entrusted them with responsibility for item and to stranger making a good case to take it off them ('Stranger at the Door').
• *Incentive* – perhaps picnickers will be allowed to continue if only they can convince the farmer that they know how to behave appropriately in the country ('Country Code').
• *Turning tables* – pirates grab at the treasure chest that has been the purpose of their quest, only to discover that anyone taking it into their possession becomes stricken with the 'curse of frozen tongue' ('Pirates').
• *Surprise* – new recruit to factory (teacher in role) suddenly starts disrupting and behaving inappropriately in the work situation ('The Factory').
• *Abdication* – responsibility for the outcome invested in one person: will the parcels contain Roberta's hat, as each is unwrapped in turn by a member of the group? ('Roberta').
• *Appropriate action* – new recruits to hospital team are urged to keep appropriately on task by the person in charge ('Teamwork').
• *Ritual* – each member of pirate band expresses solidarity and allegience by raising hand in 'Black Spot' salute ('Pirates').

- *Daring/Challenge* –
(a) at the start of the lesson, teacher wonders whether the group will be able to do the kind of drama she has in mind ('The Factory');
(b) within the drama, picnickers are challenged to answer angry farmer's questions correctly ('Country Code').
- *Limitation* –
(a) of a vital necessity – 'How are we to survive in this place?', the pirate chief asks fellow survivors of the shipwreck ('Pirates');
(b) of space – teddy bears squashed together in close proximity in their show cases ('Teddy Bear Museum');
(c) of time – only a few days left before the contractors arrive, to alert public attention to the proposed destruction of conservation woodland ('Theme Park').

Tension of contrast

This can help give integrity to the drama through the *way* something happens. This is particularly valuable with pupils with special educational needs, in giving structure and helping the 'ebb and flow' of the drama, keeping pupils 'on task' through surprise at changes in mood, and keeping the attention of those pupils whose concentration is apt to wander. Certain drama conventions by their very nature will bring tension when used in juxtaposition, such as structured play contrasted with freeze frame (see the next section – 'Drama Conventions').

- *Darkness/light* – dark at night when the teddies come alive; light by day when the teddies are still ('Teddy Bear Museum').
- *Silence/sound* – the calm before the storm ('Pirates').
- *Stillness/movement* – one day we see 'Roberta' in her garden; the next day all is quiet ('No Answer').
- *Use of space* –
(a) following wild shipwreck (moments of freedom), survivors gather together round the campfire (expression of solidarity) ('Pirates').
(b) after sitting comfortably on seats in the 'bus', the children have to sit on the floor as they squash up on the picnic rug ('Country Code').
- *Use of voice* – serene tones at the picnic suddenly disturbed by the gruff voice of angry farmer ('Country Code').
- *Use of pace* – a fast activity contrasted with a slow one: ward team carrying out routine tasks are suddenly thrown into state of emergency ('Teamwork').

Tension from symbols
- *Action* –
(a) new employee in factory starts messing around and upsetting the factory floor ('The Factory');
(b) pirate chief (teacher in role) slowly and deliberately removes headband and throws it on the ground, to indicate to fellow shipwreck survivors that he or she no longer feels they can be in charge ('Pirates');
(c) friendly stranger offers sweets to school party on ferry ('Stranger Danger').
- *Music* – request song to Maggie May mentions items required for picnic ('Maggie May').

- *Object* –
(a) shipwreck survivor places the salvaged pirate flag amidst the circle of pirates, symbolic of their own survival ('Pirates');
(b) tatty box apparently contains the secrets of the island ('Pirates').
- *Picture* – RSPCA official shows picture of missing animal – has anyone seen it? ('Stranger at the Door').
- *Letter* – Mr Bear (teacher in role) opens letter he has received that morning – what will it say? ('Lucky').
- *Words* – pirates utter 'Black Spot' as reminder of their pledge of commitment ('Pirates').
- *Teacher in role* – pupils have dressed teacher in role as Mary, but she looks sad ('Birthday Presents').

Drama Conventions

Drama exercises

These are short-term, clear-cut, tightly structured activities, therefore necessarily limiting in a creative sense. These activities can be particularly useful for reaching mixed-ability groups, as they have appeal at many different levels of ability, particularly physical or musical tasks, and so can bring the whole group together within the drama. They are also good for children with short concentration spans, as they provide a clear focus for attention.

- **Drama games** can be used as warm-up activities (eg, 'Farmer Bailey' game in 'Country Code' drama, passing the hat round and imitating his voice and actions).
- **A Prescribed Drama Structure** can be contextualized as part of the on-going drama (eg, creating the teacher in role as Roberta in 'No Answer').
- **A ritual** will bring together the whole group and reaffirm group allegiance and commitment in a common action (eg, 'Black Spot' ritual in 'Pirates').
- **Movement experiences** can be used, as a warm up (see 'Stranger Danger') or contextualized within the drama (eg, pirates crawl through island vegetation, symbolized by body shapes – 'Pirates').
- **Cross-curricular tasks,** such as social skills and language work may be contextualized within the drama, giving pupils an opportunity to transfer and apply learning in a meaningful context (eg, relating a picture to a concrete object in the 'Maggie May' Prescribed Drama Structure; learning to say 'No' in 'Stranger Danger').
- **Rehearsal** – practising a skill to be used later in the drama – is particularly valuable for pupils with special educational needs, allowing them to try out skills before they need them, so minimizing the possibility of 'failure' or having to stop the drama (eg, tasks carried out by hospital staff checked at 'induction' before being allowed on the ward – 'Teamwork').
- **Cross-arts activities** can also become integral to the drama; egs, picture making (drawing presents for Mary – Birthday Presents'); music/singing ('Roberta', 'Aunty Glad', 'Maggie May'); writing a diary ('Pirates'); composing a letter (eg, to protest about work conditions, or to campaign); devising a song (eg, an advertising slogan or ditty); devising a dance (eg, to cheer someone up, or as a ritual); mime skills ('Mr Bailey').

Structured play

This is close to make-believe play; open-ended, spontaneous with a 'living through' character. The teacher organizes who is doing what and where by questioning the pupils, and may help pupils deepen their belief and commitment further by questioning them about their role. For pupils with special educational needs, questioning of individual pupils will be crucial, and may have to be very tight in order to give the pupils a very clear, narrow focus. This may seem a paradox, in that questioning may be thought to open out thinking; with many pupils with special educational needs however, the frame may have to be limited to enable them to make a creative choice or decision. For example, in a drama based on Red Riding Hood, I involved the pupils in setting the context for the drama – the pupils were to be villagers at the edge of the forest, and the drama would take place one typical morning in the village. One pupil decides that she is shopping. . . 'show me where the shop is? What is for sale in the shop? What do you want to buy? What will you do with it?' etc. In this way, the pupil's belief in what she was doing was deepened, narrowed and yet sharpened. It may take quite a while to establish context in this way and to work through all the pupils in a group. This strategy can only be useful, therefore, for those groups that are relatively small (with a maximum of ten pupils), and which have the necessary social skills and concentration spans to focus their attention and maintan commitment. Constant cross-checking between group members will be essential to maintain concentration.

Improvisation – pairs/group work

This convention places considerable demands and responsibility on pupils. Tasks need to be clear-cut and well within the social and dramatic competence of the group. Tasks should serve a purpose: to provide more information, deepen thinking and feeling, provide a change in pace, open alternative points of view or perspectives to be explored further. . . . This convention can present difficulties with control, with the risk of stereotypes being overworked and negative group dynamics between individuals – for example, it was difficult to prevent the well-meaning mainstream pupils from dominating group work with their peers with severe learning difficulties ('Stranger Danger').

For many pupils with special educational needs, the demands of this convention may well be beyond their abilities. However, this is not always the case, and may be worth trying. Often, it is not that pupils cannot engage in make-believe, but rather they lack the drive or ability to keep it going. It may be possible, therefore, for the teacher or member of staff or more able pupil to join a group, maybe whilst the others watch (eg, making a phone call in 'No Answer') or take turns to have a go at solving a particular problem (eg, the 'Stranger Danger' lesson culminated in individual pupils dealing with a teacher in role as an over-familiar stranger whilst the others watched and 'doubled', speaking advice to their friend with hand on shoulder).

Short spontaneous improvisation as a whole group is usually within the grasp of many pupils with special educational needs, provided that the teacher is able to ask questions either in or out of role, to give pupils focus and enable them to dredge up their resources to contribute to the drama.

Narrative

Storytelling

This convention can be used to stimulate the drama, for example at the start of the 'Lucky' drama, I told the popular children's story *Peace At Last* to the mainstream nursery class in question, which we then subsequently developed. Generally, however, pupils with special educational needs have difficulty concentrating on and assimilating a verbal flow. In the lesson mentioned, I told the story in vivid theatrical style to help maintain their attention, moving around and even acting out parts of it, avoided abstract ideas and concepts. Pupils with special educational needs may well need a story supported by visual images – props, felt-board (eg, Cinderella lesson with physically and sensory-impaired children, based on 'Aunty Glad' Prescribed Drama Structure), or picture-book with large clear images (eg, *Peace At Last* in the above example). An effective way of using story as stimulus with pupils with special educational needs is to involve them in a retelling of the story, with quick cross-checking to keep pupils on their toes and to ensure that everyone is 'with it'.

'Teacher hangover technique' (as coined by David Sheppard, 1991)

This is a favourite convention of mine and one which I have found particularly effective with pupils with special educational needs. The teacher deliberately stumbles over a phrase, apparently with the necessary words on the tip of the tongue or having slipped the mind altogether, so that the pupils help out by filling in the gaps. This is often very successful in eliciting elements of language from pupils, and can be targeted at an individual child working on a particular aspect of language.

Narrative links

As with storytelling, when this convention is used with pupils with special educational needs, it has to be succinct and unwordy. It can be particularly useful as teacher-talkover, to give structure and move the drama on – eg, 'the ship-wrecked pirates swam to the shore and crawled exhausted on to the beach' ('Pirates'). It can also be used to link scenes – 'the next day a special visitor arrived' ('Teddy Bear Musuem'), and move the drama forwards or backwards in time.

Theatre

This convention involves using elements of dramatic art to encapsulate meaning and sharing it through presentation to other members of the group, with a variety of styles and forms possible. It does not imply a large-scale production before an invited audience. Moments of theatre can be very useful for moving the drama on, especially if time is limited. This convention can involve quite complex conceptual grasp as well as social skills in cooperation, and may well be beyond many pupils with special educational needs as 'actors'. However, elements of theatre may be employed very effectively with pupils as 'observers', by the teacher in role or with staff supporting certain pupils. The convention can be very useful in focusing attention, and as such may also be a handy 'control' device!

• *Making a phone call* (as in 'No Answer').
• *Reading a letter* (as in 'Lucky' Prescribed Drama).
• *Tableau/frozen picture/photograph* – eg, small groups of first-school pupils worked together to demonstrate a case of exhibits in the 'Teddy Bear Museum'.
• *Small rehearsed improvisation* – eg, in the 'Pirate' drama, small groups worked together to demonstrate how the pirates managed to obtain basic vital necessities.

Football tactics

Exposure to, if not overkill by, the surfeit of sport on the television has at least benefited the drama teacher in certain respects! Generally, even pupils with severe learning difficulties seem able to grasp readily certain strategies at the football commentator's disposal; these prove valuable in enabling the pupils to gain a 'handle' on confronting the make-believe.

Action replay

Through this convention, pupils are given a second chance to do a scene. It is possible to stop the drama, maybe rehearse or practise a vital skill, before going back and trying again. It is particularly valuable for the teacher of pupils with special educational needs therefore, who may need to find many such opportunities for the pupils to practise applying a particular skill. It is also highly useful in re-presenting a point in the drama, so enabling slower pupils to 'catch up' with what is happening. It can be useful too, in recapping a scene from a previous session, perhaps where a drama is carried over two lessons (as with the song used to link the 'Pirates' rolling drama).

Slow motion

This can be useful as a control device, as in the potentially explosive situation of a shipwreck ('Pirates' drama). It can also be used to heighten pupils' awareness of their actions and reactions. However, many pupils with special educational needs may find extreme difficulty in exerting such mental, let alone physical control and coordination. Slow motion can be used quite effectively with pupils with special educational needs, however, as an element of 'theatre', the pupils perhaps watching a teacher in role and attempting to read body language and to interpret the person's state of mind (eg, watching Roberta unwrap the parcels in the 'Roberta' Prescribed Drama Structure).

Freeze frame

At the high point of a piece of improvised action, the teacher may call 'freeze', like pausing the video. Pupils with special educational needs are unlikely to be able to hold the necessary physical or mental concentration for long however, but this strategy nevertheless can have its uses. For example, it may be a control device at a high point of excitement in a group improvisation. It may also be used to heighten pupils' awareness of a moment of tension, especially if followed by questioning them about the drama at that point, as in 'Stranger Danger', where the pupils had to anticipate what the child should say to the hassling stranger. It can also be used to move the drama on, halting the action and pausing, perhaps with a teacher narrative link, before considering the next scene.

Teaching by 'negative role'

This is an extremely useful convention with pupils with special educational needs. It entails doing the opposite of what one would expect: for example, deliberately shouting loudly and moving abruptly when approaching a frightened animal (see 'Lucky' Prescribed Drama). Pupils are struck by the incongruity of the situation. Many pupils with special educational needs may not be able to think of a suggestion to resolve a particular situation, but are able to identify what *not* to do. Using a negative role model often prompts them to make connections and to show a more constructive approach by correcting you, even if they are unable to articulate it.

Teacher-in-role

This is easily the drama teacher's most valuable tool, particularly for working with pupils with special educational needs. Whilst it does beg acting skills in a sense, that does not imply going for an Oscar or a Larry! Rather, it is a mantle or teaching tool to enable the teacher to enter the make-believe and convey signals or meaning in process. The teacher can then manipulate and structure the drama from within, without breaking the fictitious context being created. The teacher needs to avoid 'hamming it up', as this will be distracting – taking it seriously will help give a legitimizing effect on the pupils ('If teacher is doing it, then it must be ok'!). When working with pupils with special educational needs, the teacher-in-role will need to make signals clear and blatant to convey meaning through the role; subtlety or unclear signals may well go completely over their heads. Using simple props will help indicate that the teacher is entering the make-believe; again, just the bare minimum is required, otherwise pupils may think they are watching entertainment or pantomime.

Uses of teacher-in-role are well documented by Cecily O'Neill and Alan Lambert (1982) and by Geoff Davies (1983). Notably for. . .
- *Moving pupils quickly into the drama* – eg, 'Good morning everyone, thank you for coming here today' (spoken as the hospital administrator in 'Teamwork').
- *Presenting an opposing view-point* – eg, 'I don't want a museum full of teddy bears; no one's interested in them any more' (spoken as prospective purchaser of the building housing the 'Teddy Bear Museum').

• *Providing a focus for attention* – eg, 'Roberta' being dressed according to the items revealed in packages opened by the group.

• *Providing an appropriate model for behaviour* – eg, 'Thank goodness you're safe' (spoken appreciatively as pirate chief, as he or she warmly greets other survivors of the shipwreck – 'Pirates').

• *Presenting challenges* – eg, 'Your ball has damaged my garden; I'll think about giving it back, if you can find a way to make it up to me . . .' (spoken as angry neighbour, 'Mr Bailey').

• *Multiplying options within the drama* – by gaining an extra person and another life-style – moving in and out of role and changing roles if the usefulness of one becomes obsolete, maybe transferring it to a pupil; eg, switching roles from the child to the stranger in 'Stranger Danger', and transferring role to a pupil (indicated by change of simple prop to denote).

The teacher has to find an appropriate role to operate inside the drama and manipulate it from within, whilst empowering the pupils to contribute ideas.

• **Low status** – someone in need of the group's expertise; eg, Lucy (teacher in role) needing to know how to look after Lucky, her animal.

• **High status** – an authority figure who impels respect, control or a correct response/appropriate behaviour; eg, the pirate chief in the 'Pirates' drama.

• **An agent** – someone carrying out orders or instructions, who may become a potential ally for the group.

• **A stranger** – someone to whom the group are obliged to explain themselves; eg, a journalist at the scene of a demonstration ('Theme Park').

• **Indeterminate role** – which may become clear-cut later on; eg, Mr Wilson who wanders into the factory after a job as a means to consolidate the children's ideas and belief about their role and their jobs; later on as the drama develops, this character becomes instrumental in confronting their attitude to responsibility ('The Factory').

Additional Teaching Strategies

Stopping the drama

This strategy needs to be used very selectively with pupils with special educational needs: not only do you risk losing a make-believe context that is carefully and often painstakingly being created, but you also risk confusing pupils by switching in and out of role. A simple prop such as a hat or cloak can help prevent confusion by making it clear when the teacher is talking in or out of role; another way is to talk the pupils through it if necessary – 'I'm not being Melanie now, remember when I wear this shawl, I'm pretending to be the owner of the Teddy Bear Musuem'. This strategy can help youngsters with special educational needs to understand how make-believe works and their capacity to offer ideas and be creative, thereby also helping to sustain their attention by reinforcing the notion of *their* drama. It will help sharpen their awareness of doing something 'one step removed', so enabling them to learn from the drama medium: doing drama and watching themselves doing it at the same time.

Stopping the drama can be useful as a quick cross-check to make sure everyone is 'with' the drama – the teacher stops the drama briefly (removing hat) before resuming role, to ask quickly, 'Who was I pretending to be? Who do you think you were? Why were you being congratulated?'. It can also be the ultimate threat and control device. Stopping the drama can also be valuable if the drama feels it is up a blind alley: in the 'Pirate' drama for example, I turned the onus back on the children to decide what direction the drama should take next – suggestions were chalked on a board and a vote taken. Also, stopping the drama at a high point in the action can leave the pupils wanting more, or wanting to know more, and so can be a useful means for generating a sense of enquiry in pupils with special educational needs – particularly if the teacher finds him or herself unsure how to structure the conclusion to the lesson!

Questioning

Closed questions
Closed questions are those demanding a Yes/No answer, and have specific application and usefulness. Closed questions must be used selectively as they do not generally demand a creative response, and can be limiting. Paradoxically, however, they may have considerable scope in empowering pupils with special educational needs. The skill depends on the teacher, in phrasing a question such that a pupil may be able to indicate Yes/No in response; such a decision may affect that pupil's whole contribution to the drama. For example, in a version of the 'Aunty Glad' Prescribed Drama Structure, conceptually able but physically impaired pupils were able to indicate a preferred task to assist Cinderella. Such questions may also be used strategically by the teacher, to work on group dynamics or the 'social health' of the group or to elevate the status of a particular pupil; such a decision may affect that pupil's contribution to the drama and may even change the whole course of the action. Closed questions can thus be a valuable tool for working with pupils with special educational needs, and may be used in different ways.

• *As a quick cross-check of facts* – 'did you think he (or she) – the new owner of the Teddy Bear Museum – was a nice person?'
• *To create a sense of urgency* – 'You will help me get my ball back, won't you?'
• *To gain attention* – 'Have you seen Lucky?'
• *To remind about the task in hand* – 'That's how you go up to a frightened animal, isn't it?'
• *To gain consensus* – 'Do you think we should go to Roberta's house, then?'
• *To empower* certain pupils to make a creative decision – 'Shall we go in - yes or no?'.

Open questions
In drama, there will often be situations where there may not be a 'right' answer and the teacher will be looking to empower the children and

maximize opportunities for their decision making through the use of 'open questions'. These should be well within the pupils' grasp: eg, 'How can we move so that no one will hear us?', 'How can we make our plan better?', 'What do we know about this person?'. The drama teacher working with pupils with special educational needs should retain the notion of challenging the group: he or she may begin with an open question, but in order to enable a pupil to gain a clear focus within the drama, follows the original question with subsequent ones that increasingly narrow the parameters of thought, maybe working towards a closed question – remember, a Yes/No answer may still have the capacity to alter the direction of the drama.

Discussion and reflection

Discussion

This is a useful strategy for consolidating and clarifying ideas, although it can easily become boring, tedious, overworked and confusing. It can be very useful for slowing down the drama, for pupils to think through the implications of a situation rather than rushing headlong – eg, 'What should we take with us into the woods, in our search for Red Riding Hood?'.

- *Beforehand* – eg, 'What do you think of when I say the word "pirate" to you?'
- *In role, as part of the on-going drama* – eg, 'What should we take with us on our picnic?'
- *Afterwards* – beware the classic overkill: 'What was our drama about today?', which can be deadly. However, discussion after the drama may be critical in putting distance, and in enabling pupils to distinguish between the make-believe and the real world, and to transfer and generalize learning from the drama to their real life experience (eg, 'Stranger Danger' lesson).

Reflection

This is important in consolidating learning both after the drama and also whilst the drama is in process. The teacher of pupils with limited verbal powers will have to find alternative ways to bring their attention to a significant moment.

- *Pausing the action momentarily* – eg, 'Let us close our eyes for a moment and remember our pirate friends who did not survive the shipwreck ' ('Pirates').
- *A diary entry* – eg, life aboard ship ('Pirates').
- *A ritual* – eg, shaking hands on successful appointment to the hospital team ('Teamwork').
- *A report or letter* to be delivered in the drama – eg, a protest letter ('Theme Park').
- *Drawing a picture afterwards* – eg, of the ward team in the hospital ('Teamwork').
- *Writing afterwards* – eg, letters from mainstream pupils to their friends in the SLD school, reminding them of ways to be streetwise ('Stranger Danger').

- *Playing out some of the events* from the drama in the playground or home-corner situations.

Unfortunately none of these strategies is completely bullet-proof! Problems do arise, and the teacher working in drama with pupils with special educational needs may be under considerable pressure to hold it all together, since the pupils may not be able to take responsibility to help resolve a quandry. What can you do if it feels like it's all going wrong? The next chapter attempts to offer some constructive suggestions – trouble-shooting, in other words!

CHAPTER 6

Troubleshooting! – some 'golden rules' for drama with pupils with special educational needs

This chapter considers common difficulties when working in drama with pupils with special educational needs, and possible ways of dealing with these challenges. Some were originally identified by John Taylor (1984, 1986a and b); the rest are my own observations and those of teachers with whom I have worked. I offer 'golden rules' by way of key strategies for the prospective te.cher of drama in the field of special educational needs. They have all at times been useful pointers for my own practice, so I hope they work for you!

Present tasks boldly and simply

• *Limit the amount of listening* necessary: pupils may not be able to assimilate a verbal flow.
• *Work immediately in role* to reduce the necessity for complex language structures: 'What would you do if. . .' can become immediately translated into the here-and-now.
• *Find ways to repeat* or paraphrase instructions several times, to give pupils a chance to 'catch up' with the action.
• *Ask 'real' questions* within the pupils' grasp.
• *Cross-question* and cross-check to ensure everyone is 'with' the drama.
• *Strategically place pupils with sensory disabilities*, eg, ensure that pupils with hearing loss can see you.
• *Have a clear focus* and sense of purpose.
• *Retain the notion of challenging the pupils*, eg, give them the opportunity to answer an 'open' question, but be prepared to narrow the focus, maybe even working towards a 'closed' question. Remember: a Yes/No answer may have the power to alter the direction of the drama if the question is posed appropriately.

Circumvent difficulties of limited conceptual framework

• *Work from the 'concrete'* first to give clear focus for make-believe, then supply the abstract term; don't move on too fast – be prepared to refer back to the 'concrete'.
– create/enact the scene physically, blocking the area with furniture or

props and demarcating it with chalk lines or masking tape, then ascribe it as the 'beach', 'village', etc.;

– supply role-names once pupils can associate this with something 'concrete': establish the windmill, the place where corn is ground into flour, and identify the person who does this job, then refer to him or her as 'the miller';

– give the pupils an experience before applying the abstract word for it, eg, 'surprising': precede with a genuinely-felt turn of events.

• *Paradoxically limit the structure of the drama:* ensure that parameters are clearly defined within which the pupils are required to make choices and decisions, and well within the pupils' capability; although this may seem limiting in a creative sense, it will actually enable them to engage in divergent thinking by giving a clear focus for creative thought.

• *Build up the drama in very small increments:* create the drama step by step, if necessary talking the pupils into the make-believe; eg, 'When I put this hat on, I won't be talking to you as Melanie any more, I'll be pretending to be somebody else. . .'.

• *Make the drama relevant to the group's experience:* this can be broadened through use of teacher-in-role (accessible and direct); remember too, that pupils' worldliness is necessarily extended by familiarity with TV (*Star Trek, Thunderbirds, Neighbours* – Australia, etc.), which increases possible options for drama themes.

Avoid pupils 'switching off'

• *Use their ideas and initiatives,* however small – a choice or decision may not actually affect the structure of the drama, but will nevertheless enrich it and add colour (adding meat to the bones); the pupils will sense this, and care more about what is apparently *their* drama.

• *Make suggestions coherent:* it may be necessary to relate an idea back to the *intention* and rephrase it; eg, 'How can we cheer Cinderella up?'; 'Sweep' answers a child, pointing at a broom – 'Ah! You think we should help her do her jobs?!'

• *Take the drama seriously* – reject an idea, *not* the child.

• *Work in role to legitimize the activity* – 'It must be ok if teacher does it!'

• *'Model' appropriate emotional engagement* through use of teacher-in-role.

• *Use props to indicate when in role;* this will help avoid confusion.

• *Adopt a multi-sensory approach,* not only as a stimulus, but in responding to and reinforcing the pupils' initiatives.

• *Use 'focusing' devices:* attractive objects/stimuli, music/songs, teacher-in-role, moments of 'theatre', etc.

• *Teach that actions have implications* through strategies of rehearsal and repetition, adding to the drama in small increments; this will help avoid pupils getting carried away in excitement;

• *Consider stopping on a high note or cliff-hanger* – very useful for generating a sense of enquiry in pupils with special educational needs, and also if the teacher finds him or herself unsure how to conclude or resolve a drama!

Manage mixed-ability groups

- *Aim to reach all the people some of the time.* Invariably this will at times entail working at the level of the most/least able, or somewhere in the middle; alternatively, possibly consider 'streaming' classes for drama.
- *Include tasks that can be enjoyed at many levels of ability:* eg, a Prescribed Drama Structure, a ritual, drama game, music, movement, a physical task, etc.
- *Use a Prescribed Drama Structure flexibly:*
  - to elicit responses at different levels of engagement within the make-believe;
  - contextualized in open-ended drama to challenge pupils at all ability levels;
  - with others in succession on a theme, to make a Prescribed Drama event.
- *Work to people's strengths:* eg,
  - *as an observer* (for a child who uses a wheelchair or an insecure child, consider a role with low exposure but high status, eg, the one who judges whether the would-be recruits are suitable);
  - *as a leader* (possibly for a relatively bright pupil, create a strong role that helps or challenges, to make a link with others).
- *Ensure that all pupils contribute* to the drama, however small the idea.
- *Keep a stock of simple objects and pictures:* use visual images to support the spoken word, to access 'meaning' to pupils at different levels of conceptual symbolic understanding.
- *Be aware of group dynamics* and opportunities to raise the status of certain pupils in the eyes of their peers: a small decision (Yes/No) could potentially have the power to change completely the direction of the drama, or at least affect its outcome.
- *Work to the strengths of additional staff* – brief as fully as possible ahead of the session; target certain staff to work alongside and support particular pupils, as necessary.

Find ways to 'contain' the pupils

- *Constrain the use of space:* masking tape, chalk demarcations, blocking with furniture, etc.
- *Hide props* – keep concealed and out of reach if necessary.
- *Include static strategies:* moments of 'theatre', 'frozen pictures', etc.
- *Consider incorporating a structured activity,* such as a drama game or exercise (song, picture, movement, etc.).
- *Incorporate physical tasks* to help channel surplus energy!
- *Ensure that there is a flow and change of type of activity:* this will enable those with short concentration spans to 'come and go' and focus their attention better.
- *Include elements with strong visual impact:* eg,
  - use of attractive objects;
  - teacher in role with props (NB not too many as this may be bewildering and bemusing – just enough to indicate a change in persona);
  - use of face-paints or make-up (NB used selectively, for reasons above).
- *Use contrast to give tension and surprise and keep them 'on task':*
  - in lighting (light/dark);
  - in sound (quiet/noisy);

– in pace (fast activity, then slow down);
– in use of space ('free' eg, structured play, then back to group, eg, meeting in a circle);
– in voice (sudden loud tones, then quiet).

• *Greet everyone individually by name* (in a name song?) at the start of the lesson: this will help establish group cohesion and raise self-esteem, as well as emphasizing that everyone is being valued as an individual. It will give the group a chance to focus on you and get used to you (especially if you are not their regular teacher) and give you the opportunity of learning as many names as possible – a moment's hesitation later on may lose you the drama if momentum is lost and concentration broken, and enable you to deal quickly and efficiently with individuals!

• *Challenge the pupils,* both before the drama starts, and during it, in order to establish commitment and consensus for the make-believe. For example:

– 'I'm not sure you'll be able to do this drama today. . .'
– 'I normally only do this drama with older children. . .'
– 'Do you think you're up to doing something quite difficult in drama today?'
– 'Yes, I think perhaps you're ready for something quite difficult. . . what do you think? Shall we see if you are?'
– 'Oh dear, perhaps you're not able to do this after all. . . . You are? Well show me, then. . .'.

Anticipate management difficulties

• *Check timings:* timetables, commitments (speech/physio/music therapy), likely disturbances (traffic through the drama space), children needing to be toiletted at regular intervals, bus times for pupils, etc.
• *Allow sufficient time* to 'warm up' and get into the drama, and a flexible amount of time at the end for the drama to develop with still enough time to de-role and 'wind down' (very important with pupils with special educational needs, to make the distinction between the make-believe and the real world).
• *Check commitments of available staff,* who may be required elsewhere at some point during the session.
• *Minimize disturbances as far as possible* – negotiate use of space with other staff in the school.
• *Maximize the resource of additional staff,* for working alongside certain pupils who may need extra support for various reasons, or who may be apt to wander.

Establish a clear make-believe context

• *Explain to the pupils what is going on:* talk them into the drama – use the word 'pretend', eg, 'Let's pretend this cardboard box is a TV'.
• *Let the pupils watch you going into role* (getting ready), and/or let them be actively involved in dressing you or advising you on your role – do not attempt to delude them in the make-believe: they will either think they are watching pantomime, or else believe it is real, and then lose the potential for learning through drama 'one step removed'.

• *Start your session where they are used to sitting as a group* (in a circle on chairs, on a 'story mat', etc.), to give security and sense of the 'real world' to contrast with the drama.

• *Involve pupils in adapting the area,* moving the furniture to create the space for the drama – this may take a while, but it will help them into the symbolism, and allow the 'slower' pupils to 'catch up' with what is happening.

• *Ensure plenty of time to de-role:* explain that we will now 'stop the drama', involve the pupils in helping you off with hats/props and returning the furniture to its usual place; finish the lesson where they began (on chairs in a circle, sitting on the 'story carpet', etc.).

• *Talk about the drama* – 'When we were pretending just now'; whilst discussion after the lesson can be deadly, especially if the pupils are tired, it is worth at least making some reference to the lesson to insert some distance and establish the 'here and now'.

Persevere with developing proficiency in role

• *Start small:* a few minutes even, perhaps at the end of a story. Ask the pupils if they would like to meet one of the characters, and speak to them as that character, presenting bits of the story from their point of view.

• *Prop the role:* use an uncomplicated, manageable item to indicate when in and out of role. This will enable you to come out of role easily if you need to break the fiction to deal with a management problem or to clarify a point. Going over the top with props will risk distracting the pupils into watching a spectacle.

• *Explain to the pupils when the make-believe will start,* eg, 'When I put this hat on, I'll be pretending to be someone else', and make it obvious in your stance, voice and body language, without going over the top!

• *Avoid hamming up the role:* it is simply a 'mantle' for talking as someone else.

• *Be prepared to laugh with them, at first!* It is quite likely that pupils will find your 'acting' amusing the first time you try. Be positive: at least they recognize that a change has taken place! Aim then to get them to take it seriously; work to establish consensus and commitment, before doing an action replay.

• *Let the pupils advise you:* confess your inadequacies ('Oh dear. I really wasn't any good, was I?. . . How can I be the king in a way that won't make you laugh?. . . Help me act the king better. . .'). This way, the pupils will have more investment in you, and hopefully will be more likely to give you a go.

• *Be prepared to stop briefly and check how you're doing* ('Am I playing the king ok now?. . . More angry looking? ok. . .'). However, beware – this can easily become overworked and confuse pupils if you keep nipping in and out of role.

• *Take your role seriously: deal with management difficulties in role as far as possible,* eg, 'There is laughing in my monastery. This must stop at once!' (spoken as abbot). Try to come out of role to deal with disruption as a last resort.

• *Keep your signals clear and blatant:* straightforward, accessible emotions, deliberate actions and gestures.

- *Keep your talk in character,* but succinct with clear purpose.
- *Don't get stuck:* if the role has exhausted its usefulness, come out of role (take off prop, and explain 'I'm going to stop being the king now. . .'), and change to a different strategy. Maybe transfer the original role to a pupil if the character still needs to be on the scene but not necessarily so proactive.
- *Experiment with different kinds of role:* someone in authority, someone in need of help, etc. You may find you feel more at ease in a certain kind of role. Start with the thin end of the wedge and gain some confidence at negotiating and talking in that kind of role, before pushing yourself to take on different kinds of role.
- *Keep a stock of basic adaptable hats and simple props:* eg, peaked official's cap, straw hat (unisex!), a lady's 'best' hat, a man's cap, fur hat (fake) for going into role as a creature; large pieces of material (potential cloaks), scarves, shawls, glitzy glamorous scarves, walking sticks, etc.
- *Know your strengths:* if you feel desperately uncomfortable in a 'character' role, maybe harness or exploit the skills of colleagues who feel more at ease. Adopt the same principle, talking the pupils through what is happening ('In a moment Mrs Bryan will be pretending to be someone else. She will be the king', etc.). That will enable you to take a role closer to real life, alongside the pupils perhaps, who may be playing 'themselves' but caught up in a fiction.

Work to pupils' strengths and interests

- *Ask the pupils to suggest a theme* for the drama ahead of the lesson. Not only will this give you thinking time, but also help motivate the pupils and establish consensus.
- *Establish collective agreement for the drama at the outset* – even if that means deferring a particular pupil's alternative suggestion (a theme for the next lesson?). It may be necessary to compromise an individual for the sake of the group.
- *Be prepared to trust to their initiative* – if pupils are desperate to do drama on a particular theme, it may be very hard to dissuade them! Go along with their ideas, and be on the lookout for a possible learning area to arise.
- *Aim to keep everyone 'with you' during the lesson* – strategies of questioning, cross-checking.
- *Challenge participants at their respective levels of ability* – natural leaders, good 'observers' . . .allow pupils to draw on their knowledge, skills and resources.
- *Be aware of latent strengths* – pupils may be diffident about showing their aptitude, and may need sensitive encouragement and timing to tease this out.
- *Do not prolong a scene in the drama* – be sensitive to overworking something, and be ready to move the drama on.
- *Be prepared to stop!* It is often possible to salvage a drama if you sense the pupils' interest is waning, but maybe not this afternoon – don't be a martyr to drama: occasionally it may be preferable to abandon the sinking ship!

Develop the confidence of supporting staff

• *Brief assistant staff ahead of the lesson* – explain aims and objectives and the learning areas you anticipate covering. This will enable staff to appreciate the method in the madness!

• *Keep control of the direction of the drama* – explain to staff that you will take responsibility for consolidating the direction of the drama. This will enable you to structure the negotiation process with the pupils, rather than risk it becoming the grown ups' drama.

• *Consult assistant staff ahead of the lesson.* Do they mind working in role? Are they keen to do so? Do they mind having a touch of face-paint on? Would they mind sporting a particular hat or simple prop? Staff may be more willing if they can be convinced that no one else will interrupt the lesson or see them!

• *Alleviate anxiety of supporting staff.* Explain their function ahead of the lesson and how you would like to use them. (In role? Supporting a particular pupil?). It may be necessary to brief staff to give pupils a chance to respond without their prompting at first, if you sense they may be over keen to support. If they are to work in role, explain clearly how to do it (not over the top!) and whether you wish them to speak.

• *Give clear signals to staff in process.* Develop a system of communication with supporting staff, especially when one of you is in role. Ensure you are unambiguous! Do not be worried about briefing staff as the drama unfolds – a quickly whispered instruction, or nod of the head across the room will suffice.

• *Find roles that people feel comfortable with* – staff and pupils! Staff may be fine 'in role' if this is not far removed from themselves (eg, a neighbour wanting to borrow something) and where they feel they don't have to 'act' at all. Alternatively, they may prefer to 'hide' behind a character (eg, police officer).

Ensure a worthwhile learning experience

• *Include opportunities for the following:*

– attention (see above, under 'containing pupils');
– decision making (however small);
– bringing their own knowledge and resources to the drama;
– reflection (verbal and/or non-verbal) (Dorothy Heathcote, in Wagner, 1976).

• *Keep a clear structure:* avoid getting side-tracked by the pupils' responses into exploring every possible make-believe scenario that could develop. Whilst these may be perfectly valid, being able to spot the learning potential of going off at a tangent 'on one's feet' sometimes may be daunting, especially when starting out in drama with pupils with special educational needs. Remember, you may not have the option of building in 'thinking time' later on – a moment's hesitation on your part may also prove fatal in losing the attention and concentration of the group.

• *Be prepared to take charge* of the direction of the drama at least at the outset, but with planned elements of flexibility so that the pupils still feel it is their drama ('putting the meat to the bones' at the outset perhaps).

• *By all means aim to work totally from the pupils' ideas,* depending on the learning potential of the material and their learning need or the learning area that you may wish to explore; consider, however, negotiating a topic for the drama ahead of the lesson, to gain yourself some thinking time which you may not otherwise have 'on the hoof'.

• *Be prepared to abandon an original plan* – apparently bizarre ideas may have their own weird logic. Occasionally it may be appropriate to 'block' an inappropriate suggetion, for example, if a pupil mixes up two different lessons – 'No, not Snow White, we did drama about that last week and today our drama is about the seaside'. (BEWARE, as this may be crushing for the pupil).

• *Draw out and emphasize a learning point* (eg, saying 'No' to strangers) whilst the memory of the drama is still vivid – with pupils with special educational needs, it cannot be assumed that they will spontaneously transfer and generalize learning. Talk about 'what happened in the drama, when we were pretending just now', and 'What would you do in the real world?'.

• *Have in mind a possible learning area* and context for exploring it, although be prepared to abandon it and follow the group's initiative – if this is unforthcoming or unviable however, at least you will still be able to offer a worthwhile learning experience in drama.

ENJOY YOURSELF!. . .(AND GOOD LUCK!)

APPENDIX

Examples of Drama Practice with Pupils with Special Educational Needs

Section 1 – Prescribed Drama Activities

– for developing understanding of the medium of drama

The examples as written illustrate ways to develop the understanding of drama at different levels, according to the kind of engagement demanded from the participants and the kinds of choices and decisions they are asked to make. However, in all examples I have indicated how it might be possible to adapt each activity for other levels, according to the needs of the pupils and the kind of challenge required:

- *Level 1* limited physical or verbal response
- *Level 2* active: physical response, but not necessarily verbal
- *Level 3* interactive: verbal or signing response, conceptually more demanding
- *Open-ended* instead of the expected outcome, the participants are brought to a moment of free decision within the make-believe.

I have indicated how the Prescribed Drama Structures can have their 'lid taken off' (become '*open-ended*'). In this way, an activity can serve as a bridge into more open-ended drama, where make-believe play is *challenged* and understanding deepened. I have also included some examples actually written up as open-ended Prescribed Drama activities. In many ways they ressemble a tightly planned open-ended lesson. However, they contain a very clear 'game' element at the core of the lesson, which is crucial at this stage in the development of the pupils, in bridging the gap between understanding and beginning to use the drama medium – the 'game of theatre', as coined by Gavin Bolton (1992). I think it is also helpful for the teacher in developing his or her own practice, to think of them as essentially hinging on a 'game' framework. For this reason, whilst they could have been written up as tightly planned open-ended lessons (see examples in Section 2), I have opted to describe these particular lessons according to the format of a Prescribed Drama activity.

I have also made suggestions and given examples in some cases of how I have *contextualized* Prescribed Drama activities within an open-ended drama lesson, using them as another convention (way to organize the drama) in the teacher's repertoire.

Author's note:
The activities on pages 56 to 63 were originally devised by John Taylor (1983) and termed 'drama games'. In developing them as Prescribed Drama Structures, I have elaborated on the original 'game', as described in the sections headed 'Suggestions' and 'Examples'.

Level 1   ***'CROSSING THE ROAD'***   **PRESCRIBED DRAMA**

Props
Percussion instruments; rope/masking tape/chalk; zebra crossing made out of alternate pieces of black and white sugar paper; 'vehicles' – wheelchairs or buggies.

Preparation
Use the rope/masking tape/chalk to mark a roadway in the hall or large space. Place the zebra crossing strategically across the roadway. Sit the group well back, with a member of staff – this activity can get very hectic.

Implementation
A minimum of two pupils in 'vehicles' are pushed up and down the roadway on opposite sides as fast as they dare. Bells or hooters can add to the belief, but should be kept silent at this point! The leader brings the first pupil to the zebra crossing, and encourages them to perform kerb drill whilst everyone says the rhyme:

> *(Mark) wants to cross the road*
> *Look left and right (he's) always told;*
> *Look left, look right I think it's clear. . .**
> *Vroooooom, that car came very near.*

At the point in the rhyme marked *, the pupils in the vehicles should roar down the roadway from opposite directions so that a 'near miss' is contrived – the leader pulls back the child crossing the road and maybe swings him or her round, just in time to avoid disaster. (It is important to time this right!). The incident should be accompanied by a great cacophony of sound from the vehicles and also any extra members of staff with noisy percussion (drums, cymbals, etc.). The next child then has his or her turn, and so on, also swapping the drivers of the vehicles. *John Taylor (1983)*

Suggestions
Level 2 – the leader can make a big teaching-point of how to cross at a zebra crossing: waiting for the vehicles to stop, as well as performing the kerb drill correctly. Pupils should then be allowed to cross the road as independently as possible.
Level 3 – pupils could each have a shopping bag. Leader could greet the pupils and ask them (eg) where they are going, what they are going to buy, etc., before they cross the road.
Open-ended – run activity as described, but then create a problem for the group to resolve, eg, draw attention to a purse on the ground (having been placed strategically at a suitable moment). It is full of money. What should they do? Leader or assistant could enter in role as a member of the public – he or she has lost a purse. Do they now own up and hand it back to the owner?

Examples
a) I used this activity with a very mixed-ability group of pupils with severe learning difficulties. Many had profound and multiple learning disability (PMLD), as well as demonstrating considerable

56

autistic tendencies. For these pupils, the activity afforded a secure and structured framework, within which they could come and go. The sudden bursts of sound also riveted their attention, and helped them engage in the activity. They were involved in a group experience, and shared pitches of excitement and calm. Some pupils, however, were relatively able, and could also work on road safety as a cross-curricular skill. I could therefore work on several levels at once within the structure.

b) With a group of SLD pupils, I contexualized it as part of the unfolding open-ended 'Mr Bailey' lesson, which enabled two PMLD students to be reached at their level.

| Level 2 | *'TRAIN JOURNEY'* | **PRESCRIBED DRAMA** |

Props
Tickets; ticket officer's hat; money; whistle.

Preparation
Establish an area slightly apart from the group to be the ticket office. Install the ticket officer – let the group witness the transformation as the member of staff puts on the hat. Leader explains he or she will be the engine of the train, and that the group, sitting together, will each in turn be the passengers.

Implementation
Pupils to go up one by one to buy ticket and take their place in the train (holding on to the leader at the waist). Everybody says:

> *(Gemma) wants to catch a train*
> *To (Cromer) and back again.*
> *(She) buys (her) ticket, waves good'bye*
> *The train is leaving right on time.* (blast on whistle)

The train moves off, wheelchairs and feet moving in time to sound effects. It is important that the build up and slow down of the train sound (made by the leader and available staff with percussion) must fit the rhyme that everyone says:

> *Slowly, slowly off it goes,*
> *Slowly, slowly past the rows*
> *Of houses; faster, faster, faster, faster,*
> *Faster, faster. . . then it starts to slow,*
> *(Her) friend is there to say 'Hello'*

When the train arrives, another child is there to say 'Hello', and then it is his or her turn to go on the train, thus allowing the session to flow, with the train gradually getting longer and longer! *John Taylor (1983)*

Suggestions
Level 2 – run activity as described, encouraging pupils to approach teacher in role as guard, and going through the mechanics of the activity.

Level 3 – encourage pupils to interact appropriately with teacher in role as the guard using social graces, and to greet friends in role appropriately.

Open-ended – run activity as described, but step in an assistant in role last time round as the 'friend' that the train meets the other end. Give the character a fictitious name – maybe he or she could invite them to his or her place. Contrive a problem that the pupils can resolve – he or she needs their help for some reason, eg, it's her daughter's birthday – could they each give her an idea of a suitable birthday present? etc.

Example

I used this activity with young and profoundly and multiply learning-disabled pupils in a school for pupils with severe learning difficulties. All the pupils were encouraged to interact within the make-believe, eg, to wave good'bye, with help if necessary, and to make eye-contact. The more able pupils went to the ticket office and exchanged coins for a ticket from the ticket officer (role-played by another child). More profoundly and multiply-disabled pupils bought a ticket with help, and wheelchairs took their place behind the engine.

Level 2	*'ROBERTA'*	PRESCRIBED DRAMA

Props

A teacher or member of staff to be Roberta (or Roberto); clothes which Roberta can put on, individually wrapped in colourful wrapping paper; a hat, also wrapped, but hidden apart from the other parcels; face-paints.

Preparation

Sit the group in a horseshoe-shape facing Roberta. Explain to the group that we're going to make (the member of staff) into your friend Roberta. Let the group watch as you give her bright rosy pink cheeks. Roberta does not speak – let the group say hello to her, maybe shake hands.

Implementation

Tell group that Roberta wants to go out, but she can't because the weather is too awful. Roberta shows she's fed up about that! Explain cheerfully however, that you and the children may be able to help: dramatically tip the parcels onto the floor in the middle of the group – all except the one containing the hat, which should remain hidden. Sing or say:

> Roberta's got no hat
> Roberta's got no hat
> It's raining too, you'll catch the 'flu
> You can't go out like that.

Invite a child to fetch a parcel (build in colour recognition work) and open it, and then help Roberta into the garment, naming it if the pupil is able to. Let Roberta show she is pleased. Ask 'Is it a hat?'. . .NO!. . . (Deep sigh from Roberta!). Repeat the game until everyone has had a turn at opening a parcel. Then discover the missing parcel. Choose someone to open the last parcel and provide Roberta with the hat. Roberta, grateful, could then wave good bye and go out. Involve the children in bringing back the member of staff (de-robing Roberta), as this is important learning about make-believe. *John Taylor (1983)*

Suggestions

Level 1 – use textured paper and emphasize multi-sensory elements.
Level 3 – let Roberta speak, and encourage the pupils to interact with her appropriately. Perhaps Roberta could ask them questions before she goes, eg, about their day; maybe the pupils could make her a cup of tea (pretend).
Open-ended – run activity as described, BUT maybe there is no hat. . . Roberta is very upset, can the group help? (Make a hat for Roberta? Go to 'shop' and buy her one? Improvise a hat, eg, with a headscarf?)

Examples

The repetitive song or rhyme helps give pace and structure and reinforces group feeling (the drama convention of everyone 'playing the game'), but you may prefer not to use it. The pupils' attention tends to be riveted by the spectacle of the parcels and the transformation of a member of staff – important learning about symbolism and make believe. The pupils are also beginning to relate (non-verbally or verbally) with someone in role, thus engaging and adapting their behaviour within the make-believe. The activity is of course complete in itself. However, I have frequently used it to precede more open-ended drama activity. Roberta may become a character who chances upon a problem that the group helps resolve (See level 3). Maybe change the name – frail Granny Dryden from Postman Pat? Or do it in French?

| Level 2 | *'AUNTY GLAD'* | **PRESCRIBED DRAMA** |

Props

Teacher or member of staff in role as Aunty Glad (or Uncle Sid); face-paints, simple clothing – headscarf, cap; a set of objects relating to simple tasks, eg, tea pot, iron, duster, mop, etc.; pictures of these items, mounted on felt-board if possible; masking tape; large room-divider screen or upturned table.

Preparation

Make a house for Aunty Glad using masking tape on the screen for windows, door, letterbox, etc. – involve the pupils in making these decisions as far as possible. Put all the objects inside the house. Put the member of staff playing the part of Aunty Glad in role in front of the class – pink rosy cheeks, headscarf.

Implementation

Aunty Glad enters her 'house' and sits down, fed up. She does not speak. If need be, she indicates the objects lying around. Wait for the pupils to suggest helping her. Prompt them if necessary. In turn, the pupils offer to help with a job of their choice. They may choose by showing (signing, eye-pointing) rather than actively selecting. The felt-board may be used here: the pupil makes a choice from the pictures and then has to locate the appropriate object to carry out the task. Limit the range of choice according to the ability of the pupil to make a selection – some pupils may be bewildered by a dazzling array of items. Everyone has a turn with a job; each time Aunty Glad is extremely grateful. As the pupil works, say, sing (chant or rap): (for example)

> *Ironing clothes for Aunty Glad,*
> *Swish swish swish, swish swish swish;*
> *Ironing clothes for Aunty Glad,*
> *(Michael) gets it done.*

John Taylor (1983)

Suggestions

Level 1 – pupil to select an object and use it appropriately.
Level 3 – Aunty Glad speaks. Pupils could call at the house in turn and interact with Aunty Glad appropriately. She could ask them to do a particular job – can the child select the correct item for the task and use it appropriately?
Open-ended – run activity as described, but at the end Aunty Glad is still fed up. What is the matter? Can the group help? (eg, Fed up with her lifestyle – can the group think of other kinds of jobs she could do? Can they offer advice on job interview skills? Fed up because she's not feeling well – she's hurt her foot. Can group make it better? etc.)

Examples

I have used this activity many times with various groups of pupils with learning difficulties. The rhyme is not essential to this activity, and with some groups it may inhibit further developments. It does give a repetitive, secure structure however, and I have found it particularly useful with younger pupils. I adapted and contextualized the activity with a group of young physically disabled and sensory-impaired pupils. I greeted them in role as Cinderella (wearing a tatty shawl), and talked to them about my miserable life. I showed them all the things I had to use for cleaning the house, and told them how tired and fed up I was. The children helped me do the jobs; the felt-board proved particularly useful, as the pictures could be removed and placed on their Bliss communication boards. The drama then became more open-ended: Cinderella heard footsteps (teacher in role as Ugly Sister) and pleaded not to give away that they had helped her, as her Ugly Sister would be furious. Would they tell?

| Level 3 | *'MAGGIE MAY'* | PRESCRIBED DRAMA |

Props
Teacher in role as Maggie (or Mickie) May – a sort of genie-type figure; picnic items: apple, crisps, chocolate, bread, biscuits, drink, etc. on a tray; a picture of each item – mounted on a felt-board if possible; a cymbal; a cardboard box/picnic hamper.

Preparation
Put the adult playing Maggie May into role in view of the group – involve them in helping her to put on her costume (token spangly headscarf or cloak). Maggie May conceals herself in a corner of the room or behind a screen; she has a tray or box containing the picnic items. The session leader has the empty box and pictures of the items (on a felt-board if possible).

Implementation
Tell the group that you're going to have a picnic. Open your box and show them that it's empty. Explain that Maggie May might help us get the things we want (show them the pictures on the felt-board), if everyone will join in singing and calling for her. Ask one of the pupils to look at the pictures and choose something he or she would like to have on the picnic. Then say or sing (chant or rap):

> We've got no (apples) in our box
> In our box today;
> We've got no (apples) in our box,
> Let's call for Maggie May. . .
> MAGGIE MAY! (everyone shouts)

Maggie then appears with the tray of items. The pupil then approaches her and asks (eye-points? signs?) for his or her chosen item, remembering social graces: 'Please' and 'Thank you'! The pupils should communicate their choice somehow to Maggie, with a minimum of help. He or she chooses it from the tray, or is handed it, and brings it back to the group. Then it is someone else's turn. *John Taylor (1983)*

Suggestions
Level 1 – skip the felt-board pictures: sing about an item that is on the tray and everyone call for Maggie May – child to select the item from the tray held by Maggie May as independently as possible. Emphasize multi-sensory aspects: the smell, feel, sound of the items.
Level 2 – run activity as described, but without having to 'ask' Maggie May for his or her chosen item off the felt-board: child to select item from the tray held by Maggie May.
Open-ended – run activity, but last time round maybe Maggie May doesn't appear (what could be the matter?) or else she hasn't got the required item (can they help?).

60

Examples

This activity is infinitely adaptable. At a mainstream nursery where pupils with special educational needs were integrated, I contextualized the activity within a more open-ended drama based on the popular children's story 'Whatever Next' – the children helped Baby Bear (teacher in role with a colander on my head!) to amass items for the picnic on the moon. With a group of SLD pupils, I used the activity as a means for the children to gather items for a birthday party for Roberta (see level 2). With a group of MLD pupils, we dispensed with the magic, so that pupils went to ask the shopkeeper for an item they saw in the shop window (felt-board). At a school for physically disabled pupils, Maggie May was Cinderella's Fairy Godmother – the children asked her for cleaning items to help Cinders. . . then the magic suddenly failed (open-ended drama!).

| Level 3 | 'BIRTHDAY PRESENTS' | PRESCRIBED DRAMA |

Props

A teacher in role as Mary (or Barry); a selection of dressing up items – a choice of hats and scarves; a board/screen/large sheet of paper to write on; choice of pens.

Preparation

Sit the group facing the board you're going to write on. Put the dressing up things in view of the class.

Implementation

Say: *I've got a friend. Her name is Mary.*
Draw the outline of Mary on the board. Show the clothes.
Say: *Which scarf is she wearing today? This one or this one?*
When the pupils have chosen, draw the appropriate scarf on the drawing of Mary. Continue until the class has chosen several things for Mary to wear. Tell the group that (the particular member of staff) will be Mary. Let them dress her up according to the decisions they have made. Mary then becomes sad. She does not speak. She goes out of the group. Explain to the group:
It's Mary's birthday. She's sad. She hasn't got any presents. Aah!
Ask each pupil to think of a present for Mary. Draw these on the board or paper, and put the name of the pupil beside each picture. Then say that we're going to pretend we have the presents. Invite each pupil to hide his or her present somewhere. Mary then returns. Let each pupil surprise her with the present: they could instruct Mary where to look. Have Mary play for a while with each present. Perhaps finish by singing 'Happy Birthday' to Mary. *John Taylor (1983)*

Suggestions

Level 1 – have a selection of visually stimulating items of clothing for Mary – let pupils explore the fabrics and dress Mary up. Ahead of the session, 'plant' various items as presents – things with interesting textures, smells, etc. The pupils could 'find' them each in turn, and give them to Mary.
Level 2 – run activity as described, but instead of instructing Mary where to look for hidden presents, simply let each child in turn give Mary the present he or she thought of (taking it 'off' the board).
Open-ended – Mary could invite the children to play with one of her toys. Maybe something goes wrong: eg, perhaps her new ball goes over the fence into the garden of a grumpy neighbour – Mary is distraught, can the group help get it back?

Examples

I used this activity as a follow-up to 'Roberta' (see level 2) with one group of children with severe learning difficulties: the children thought of presents they would like to give her for her birthday, and had her look for them. At a mainstream nursery where pupils with special educational needs were integrated, I adapted and contextualized the activity to fit the theme of Red Riding Hood. In role as Red Riding Hood, I asked the children for their help: I showed them my empty basket – I had forgotten presents for my Grandmother's birthday. I then asked the children to hide their presents at Grandmother's cottage, to give her a surprise. The second teacher in role as the Grandmother (playing the 'Mary' part, as above), then looked for the presents according to the pupils' instructions. This is another activity that I have used very successfully in French with pupils with special educational needs.

| Open-ended | *'STRANGER AT THE DOOR'* | PRESCRIBED DRAMA |

Props
Teacher or member of staff in role as the stranger (it is possible to manage without a second adult by explaining that you will pretend to be different people – indicate by changes of hat or simple props); a toy tea-set or real food and drink; a 'treasure': eg, a precious object, puppet representing a pet, a purse, etc.; masking tape; a room-divider screen (upturned table or back of cupboard).

Preparation
Tell the group that you'd like to invite them to your house. Use the pupils' initiatives to create the house: use masking tape on the screen to make outlines of the windows, door, letterbox, etc. ('How many windows has my house got downstairs?'; 'Is there a number on my door?', etc.). Rearrange the furniture, again using the pupils' initiatives as far as possible, to create a 'room' the other side of the screen (lounge? kitchen? etc.). Put the adult playing the stranger into role in front of the group; he or she then leaves.

Implementation
The session leader invites the class to tea. Then show the pupils your special 'treasure' – favourite pet, new birthday present, etc. Ask the group to look after it for you whilst you nip to the shops briefly (maybe you've forgotten the biscuits. . .), impressing on the pupils to take great care of it, and not to let it out of their sight. You then leave. The stranger then arrives, asking to be allowed to join in. He or she then notices the 'treasure' and cajoles the class into 'lending' it to him or her. She or he is just about to leave when you return, retrieve the treasure and send the stranger packing. Warn the children not to let in strangers and at all costs let no one touch the 'treasure'. After a few moments, find another excuse to leave. The stranger then returns again and tries to persuade the group to hand over the treasure. What do they do? The 'game' (finding a reason to leave, and a stranger enticing them to surrender the entrusted 'treasure') may be repeated several times, until the teacher feels a learning point has been grasped or that the group is ready to stop. *John Taylor (1983)*

Suggestions
Level 1 – emphasize multi-sensory elements, eg, creation of an environment as the dwelling, opportunities to handle props and respond to teacher in role, etc.
Level 2 – encourage decisions, eg, by asking 'closed' questions – 'Has my house got 4 windows? Yes or no', 'Show me where the door is'.
Level 3 – encourage interaction with teacher(s) in role as much as possible, but do not necessarily pressurize into resolving the problem.

Examples
The class may be persuaded to give up the treasure time and time again, or may quickly learn to honour their responsibilities. Go with the group's decisions, to allow them to experience the

implications of their choices. Take it seriously, so that the participants will also. A group of SLD pupils naively handed over the new birthday ball (Roberta's – see level 3). I did not attempt to persuade them to re-think at that stage. The stranger, given the ball, then lost it. The stranger and owner (Roberta) were both upset. Realizing the problem was caused by their choice of action, the players were then invited to suggest a solution: we searched for the lost item. Another time, a hungry tramp turned up, wanting items from the tea-party; this set up a genuine humane conflict. With physically disabled pupils, I used more than one stranger: a lonely old lady, and then an RSPCA official. . . should they hand the badger over?

Open-ended   **'LUCKY'**   **PRESCRIBED DRAMA**

Props
Sheet of paper and felt pens; fur coat or animal hand puppet; a hat or simple item of clothing to indicate role; member of staff to play 'Lucky' or to operate hand puppet.

Preparation
Sit the group together at one end of the room. Adult to play Lucky based also with the group initially. Have pens and paper readily available.

Implementation
Teacher, or preferably additional adult if available, starts to open drawers, cupboards, looks under tables, etc. He or she asks the pupils, 'Have any of you seen Lucky?' Wait to see what the group say or how they respond. Do they begin to join in the 'game'? Act on their initiative if appropriate/relevant. The teacher then asks the group 'Do any of you know what Lucky looks like?' Draw Lucky on the piece of paper to their specifications, or preferably involve the pupils in drawing Lucky. Ensure each child in turn contributes something and joins in the 'game'. Very often the pupils imagine Lucky to be an animal, but there is no reason why Lucky could not be a person. Put the second adult into role as Lucky in front of the group, to help the pupils in to the pretence. Show them where Lucky lives, or better still, ask the group where Lucky lives. Make a space for Lucky's 'home', using the pupils' initiatives and involvement, eg, a house – use masking tape, screen or move furniture; or a den – under a table or chair. Install Lucky in his or her home, and return the pupils back to their places. Explain to the group that 'Lucky has a problem'. Does anyone know what's the matter with Lucky? Use their initiative if relevant. If not, create a problem for Lucky (eg, needs something to eat, has hurt his or her foot, etc.). Invite the group to help Lucky, and to think through how to solve the problem. *John Taylor (1983)*

Suggestions
Level 1 – emphasize multi-sensory elements, eg, use of fur fabric to represent Lucky.
Level 2 – draw on choices and decisions as much as possible, but without pressuring to interact with Lucky; do encourage the pupils at this level to approach the teacher in role however, but give them the option of being part of the drama but at the 'edge'.
Level 3 – encourage interaction with teacher in role, but do not pressurize unnecessarily into resolving the situation.

Example
I used this activity with a mainstream nursery class where pupils with special educational needs were integrated, to create our own continuation of the popular children's story 'Peace at Last'. At the end of the story, the picture book shows Mr Bear receiving a letter: Who is it from? Teacher in role as Mr Bear read the letter to the children. It was from Mr Bear's friend Lucy: she would be calling to see them that morning. Mr Bear asked the children to help him tidy up (at this point, I built

in a version of Aunty Glad – see level 2). When all was ready, I told the children that I was going to pretend to be Lucy, and showed them Lucy's hat. I left the group and entered this time as Lucy (suitably hatted!) and started looking for Lucky. The pupils decided Lucky was a rabbit (they had a pet rabbit in their classroom). We put an unsuspecting nursery nurse student into role as Lucky under the table. I attempted to call Lucky and entice her to come out by shouting loudly (teaching by negative role). The children taught me how to look after my rabbit so that it would not run away from me again. We all then called Lucky gently, and sure enough, Lucky was persuaded to come out.

Section 2 – Open-ended Drama Lessons

– for using the medium of drama for learning

Examples of open-ended lessons in this section illustrate possible structures or lesson models according to the extent of planning ahead of the session:

- *Tightly-planned* the component activities anticipated with planned elements of freedom, with possible learning areas already in mind
- *Partially-planned* a way into the drama already anticipated, along with additional strategies to deepen belief, and several directions for the drama anticipated, although a learning area not necessarily yet apparent
- *Open* all decisions and choices concerning the direction of the drama negotiated from the outset.

The lessons illustrate examples of the above models that I have used for working in open-ended drama with pupils with differing special educational needs. In each case, I have indicated the extent of the pre-planning involved: whether a 'tightly-planned', 'partially-planned' or 'open' lesson model. I have also summarized what actually happened (successful and unsuccessful) on one particular occasion that I used the lesson plan, and attempted a rationale.

The lesson plans have been printed on separate pages, with 'what happened' in each case on the facing page. This is to facilitate easy reference and classroom use. However, the lesson plans should not be lifted and stuck to rigidly – indeed this should be impossible let alone undesirable, as any drama lesson should 'belong' to the pupils and be fed by their responses, ideas and initiatives, however small that contribution may be. Nevertheless, as Patrice Baldwin (1991. p.8) put it, lesson plans can: 'provide [flexible] frameworks for adaptation and expansion. . . [and] allow insight into other teachers' methods of working'.

Provided they are regarded in this way, and with the attitude that the outcome of any lesson should always be a 'surprise', the examples here may be useful for grasping some of the thought processes involved in teaching drama with pupils with special educational needs.

Tightly planned lesson   *'MR BAILEY'*   **Theme: NEIGHBOURS**

Aims: to develop a sense of initiative and responsibility; social skills – to deal with an angry person effectively.

Staff: two to take roles.

<table>
<tr><td>drama game stimulus</td><td>
TOPIC
Introduce Mr Bailey's hat – pass it round as we say rhyme
Mr Bailey's home today,
Mr Bailey will not play,
What does Mr Bailey say? (person holding hat stands up),
(angry) <i>Leave me alone and go away!</i>
Tell group that they may meet Mr Bailey in todays's drama (preparation for grumpy teacher-in-role).
</td></tr>
</table>

↓

<table>
<tr><td>use of space

teacher in role

theatre tension</td><td>
INITIATION PHASE
Create Mr Bailey's house using masking tape on upturned PE mat (How many windows are there? Where is the door? etc.). Use masking tape also to mark out Mr Bailey's front garden (What things are there in the garden? Where is the path? etc.).

Tell group that Mr Bailey is actually Roberta's neighbour (see level 2). Put second teacher into role as Roberta in front of group. Present Roberta with a birthday present (ball) wrapped in spangly paper. She opens parcel expectantly.
</td></tr>
</table>

↓

<table>
<tr><td>drama exercise

group improvisation</td><td>
DIAGNOSTIC PHASE
Roberta invites group to play ball game. First teacher goes into role (puts on hat) as Mr Bailey in view of the class. He is busy in his garden, and occasionally glances disgruntled at children.

Ball goes into Mr Bailey's garden. Mr Bailey is very angry and holds onto the ball. 'Leave me alone and go away!', he says. Roberta is very upset. What does the group do?
</td></tr>
</table>

↓

INTERVENTION PHASE

| group asks for ball back
– push for social graces? | group distraught
– give second chance after
warning (happens again?) | window broken
– group to make
amends? | ? |

What Happened

This lesson represented the culmination of three sessions during which we had worked through a series of Prescribed Dramas that had quite rapidly handed over more choices to the children (5–8-year olds with severe learning difficulties, eight in the group). The first week, we played 'Roberta' and 'Birthday Presents' run 'back to back' (levels 2 and 3), followed in the second week by 'Maggie May' (level 3) and a version of 'Stranger at the Door' (open-ended Prescribed Drama). Whilst with many groups one might opt to do drama activities at the same level over a period of time, this particular group had responded well to the drama conventions, and had quickly grasped what was expected of them. By this third session, therefore, I decided to take them into open-ended drama. Over the sessions, the Roberta character had provided a sense of continuity, and we had developed the theme of her birthday: assembling items for her birthday party the second week, with the help of the genie figure Maggie May, and then dealing with a series of 'strangers' at the door who were after the party things. It was logical to continue with the Roberta character into this third session, although it could just as easily have been anyone! I adapted a lesson plan originally devised by John Taylor to see to what extent this young group of children with severe learning difficulties could use their initiative within the make-believe.

teacher in role

improvisation

DIAGNOSTIC PHASE
They were highly motivated. The warm-up game proved useful preparation for teacher-in-role as Mr Bailey: they were awed but not overwhelmed or alarmed, even though I was explicitly annoyed with them. They realized it was in the make-believe. They had difficulty in coordinating a group response – a demand that was really beyond their developmental maturity, but individually they took me seriously. I used my role to give legitimation to their responses, by answering them seriously in role, even if some responses were a bit 'way off'.
The drama developed in a way that I had not fully anticipated. One child, giggling, started running across the garden, really a provocative response to the teacher in role; others were keen to imitate the action! *They needed to see the implications of their actions – a learning area!*

teacher in role

structured play

reflection

INTERVENTION PHASE
I challenged them that not only had their ball come into the garden and smashed my flowers, but now they were making things even worse by trampling on them. I insisted they each helped to make good the damage. Each in turn thought of a job in the garden (mowing, digging, pruning, weeding, etc.) and they set to work.
Mr Bailey was pleased and gave the ball back after they promised not to let it happen again! Roberta was very grateful.
Out of role, I asked them where they could find a big space to throw a ball, and we talked about going to a park.

Tightly planned lesson   *'STRANGER DANGER'*   **Theme: SAFETY**

Aims: to consolidate strategies for dealing with strangers.
Staff: two to take roles, although one would suffice, provided roles clearly denoted (props).

drama exercise –movement (warm-up) – ritual discussion	**TOPIC** a) two (mainstream) pupils make 'boat' to cradle third (SLD) pupil; b) in fours: three on hands and knees in line support fourth across their backs; gently sway to give experience of boat rocking. In circle, greet everyone and introduce yourself in Makaton signing. Introduce theme of 'boat' for today's drama: brainstorm ideas and associations on the theme.
use of space pairs/small group improvisation	**INITIATION PHASE** Explain to pupils that our drama will happen on a big boat eg, liner? ferry?. Create the areas (rearrange furniture, etc.), using pupil ideas and initiatives. Establish roles: they are to be members of school party on a trip; class teacher will be ship's officer (put into role in front of group); I will be their teacher. Prepare group that others may also join our play. In groups, pupils decide what they'll be doing on the ship, and take themselves to that part of the 'deck'. (Possibly use 'structured play' instead, if clearer focus for improvisation required).
improvisation talkover questioning teacher in role teacher in role improvisation	**DIAGNOSTIC PHASE** 'Action' – pupils to enter the make-believe. Let action run for short while, before announcement for 'school party' to assemble in cafeteria where their 'teacher' is awaiting them. Group to assemble – 'teacher' to ask them about what they've been doing and how they find the ship (deepen belief). (Responses of group? Interests? Learning area?) He or she informs group that he or she will be in their cabin if they need them. 'School party' has free time. Whilst they are enjoying themselves, 'stranger' (nice looking person) circulates and attempts to offer them sweets. What do they do?

INTERVENTION PHASE

pupils deal effectively with situation: – praised?	pupils fail to watch out: 'teacher' returns just in time: – chastises them?	pupils act promptly and report incident: – praised?	?

What Happened

This was the second lesson in a series of three integrated sessions between 11–12–year old middle school pupils and slightly younger pupils with severe learning difficulties. The mainstream pupils had poor social skills and behavioural difficulties – a high proportion were statemented. The theme for the lesson was appropriate to pupils of all levels and abilities – they were all vulnerable. I was concerned to challenge the 'nasty male' stranger stereotype, and opted for an attractive friendly female stranger. After the success of the first lesson when pupils had integrated and worked very well, I felt they were ready to handle more challenging strategies, such as pairs/small group work. It was important to retain clear structure however, as the pupils were potentially volatile and needed the security of a clear focus to enable them to create within the drama. I also needed to build in opportunities for questioning, to cross-check everyone was 'with' the drama and to deepen belief and ensure commitment all along the way, with everyone kept 'on task'.

	DIAGNOSTIC PHASE
teacher in role	When the 'stranger' appeared on the scene, pandemonium broke out: the pupils were highly charged and immediately grasped the significance of what was going on. I responded in role: I appeared from my cabin, furious with them for the noise. This of course created a tension: wrongly accused, they proceeded to explain to me in role what was happening.
rehearsal discussion	I used my role to consolidate their responses and to 'rehearse' appropriate reactions to such a stranger using their ideas and initiatives, including seeking help: I urged them to think carefully about how they had responded.
	I then returned to my cabin and the action resumed, mainstream and special school pupils integrating well within the make-believe, even though the mainstream pupils inevitably tended to dominate.
teacher in role	This second time, however, the pupils took me literally ('being aware of how they were responding'), and went for the theatrical response: we were on the verge of a death scene! *I needed to act promptly to focus on the problem and find immediate ways to resolve and deal with it.*

	INTERVENTION PHASE
theatre	I went into role as a young girl (indicated by headscarf as prop), and the group watched as the stranger approached me.
negative role pairs improvisation	I was not very effective; I transferred role to one of the pupils. The stranger approached and she began to cope well; I stopped the action however and quickly summoned another pupil to stand behind her with hand on shoulder, and speaking advice to her friend.
'doubling' theatre	I repeated this several times, swapping as many pupils as possible, mainstream and SLD.
reflection	The mainstream pupils wrote letters to SLD pupils advising about 'Stranger Danger'; the SLD pupils talked about it for days afterwards.

Tightly planned lesson   *'COUNTRY CODE'*   **Theme: THE ENVIRONMENT**

Aims: to explore notions of responsibility and atoning for behaviour; to reinforce topic work on the countryside and appropriate behaviour.

Staff: two to take roles (one may suffice, switching props/roles).

---

drama game

> *TOPIC*
> Present Farmer Bailey's hat – pass it round as we say rhyme:
> *Farmer Bailey's here today*
> *Farmer Bailey will not play*
> *What does Farmer Bailey say?* (person with hat puts it on and says)
> *Leave me alone and go away!* (angrily!)
> Tell group Farmer Bailey lives in the country – I hope we don't meet him because. . . we're going on a picnic to the country!
> (Preparation for teacher-in-role)

Prescribed
Drama

use of space

ritual (control!)

> *INITIATION PHASE*
> Show empty picnic box – we need to buy items. Play version of 'Maggie May' (level 3) to purchase items in turn from shop.
>
> Involve group in rearranging furniture to make minibus.
> Insist they enter responsibly and queue one at a time.
> Fasten seat belts – now we can go!

questioning

drama exercise.
– movement

structured play

'meeting'

teacher in role

> *DIAGNOSTIC PHASE*
> Improvise journey, eliciting individual contributions to set the scene (deepen belief). (Incident on journey. . .?)
> Arrival in country – get out of bus: lifted over stile (as high as possible) by two members of staff one at a time (tension and control device to stop them rushing headlong).
> In pairs/small groups, ask them what they'd like to do (eg, play in field, climb fence, etc.) – do not attempt to correct inappropriate suggestions at this stage.
>
> Teacher calls group over: time for the picnic. Question children about what they've been doing (consolidate make-believe). Keep atmosphere calm and pleasant (to contrast with next development – TIR puts on hat in view of group. . .).
>
> Angry Farmer Bailey enters, cross because the children have made litter, wandered off paths, left gates open, etc. (use their actual suggestions as far as possible, but do not challenge individual pupil directly). Reactions?

INTERVENTION PHASE

defend themselves?   feel guilty/responsible?   offer to atone?   ?

What Happened

The teacher of this group of 7–8–year old pupils with moderate learning difficulties had been concerned at the group's lack of self-discipline when out in the countryside recently on an educational visit. The lesson therefore was devised to provide them with a context where they would be confronted with the implications of inappropriate behaviour one step removed in the drama. It would put them in the position of having to volunteer an appropriate 'country code'. The group itself was particularly volatile – the class teacher had been working hard to reinforce social skills and consideration for others. Whilst individually they were capable of operating within the make-believe, they would need the security of a tight structure with clear focus to slow them down and consider implications at each stage as part of a group.

The lesson went according to plan, with strategies proving effective in preventing them from rushing headlong in the make-believe, which would have meant for superficiality and probable loss of control! Once in the countryside, they were eager to explore – one couple reported quicksand, but it seemed to present no obvious threat or reason to go off at a tangent at this stage, although it could have easily done so.

teacher in role

DIAGNOSTIC PHASE
I proceeded with the original plan. Some of the children started giggling. I handled this in role, and maintained my anger – even crosser now that they were laughing at me – rather than stopping and asking them to help me 'improve' my acting. One boy started to cry – not necessarily a negative sign, as this can be indicative of engagement on a feeling level; a response like this needs to be handled sensitively, however, to preserve the child's dignity. A member of staff momentarily dropped role to remind him that it was really Melanie pretending, although I could have handled this in role: 'I'm surprised the rest of you aren't crying' (elevating his status). He quickly recovered and began to make constructive contributions. The pupils quickly took it seriously in fact, and began to defend themselves. Some made excuses, said it wasn't them – one girl quite emphatically denied that she had been annoying the sheep, rather she had just been watching them. I listened to their responses, impressed by their assertiveness and attempts to get out of the fix! *I decided to make it difficult for them however, in order to focus on the 'learning area' of appropriate behaviour in the countryside.*

teacher in role

questioning

reflection

INTERVENTION PHASE
I would only let them continue picnicking on my land if they could convince me that they knew how to behave properly in the countryside. I 'tested' them, eg, 'If you saw some pretty flowers, would you pick them to take them home?', 'If you had to open a gate, would you leave it open – why not?', etc. When satisfied, I allowed them to continue their picnic.

Partially-planned lesson   *'THE TEDDY BEAR MUSEUM'*   **Theme: TOYS**

Aims: to consider notions of 'value', regardless of appearance.
Staff: two to take roles (one switching roles may suffice).

song/ritual	**TOPIC** Use teddy bear for introductory 'name song' round the circle: *Teddy went out on a bus one day and who do you think he saw?* (child fills in name) *And on he (or she) got and of they went, and who do you think they saw?* (next child). Tell pupils that the bus will stop at the Teddy Bear Museum.

discussion	**INITIATION PHASE** What is a 'museum?' What do you find there? What would be in a Teddy Bear Museum – what would it be like inside?
use of space	Rearrange furniture to create areas for the Teddy Bear Museum – use pupils' ideas and initiatives.
drama exercise	Tell group that they will be all the teddies in the museum. Can they make themselves like a teddy? Use jointed teddy – pupils to imitate poses (sitting arms outstretched, etc.).
tension	Let in on SECRET: at night the teddies come alive – the only person who knows this is the owner of the museum (preparation for teacher in role – show her shawl).

frozen picture	**DIAGNOSTIC PHASE** In small groups, 'teddies' are to make themselves into tableaux, to show how they are displayed in the museum.
questioning	Question teddies individually (deepen belief) – 'Who was your last owner? Are you holding something?', etc.
theatre/improvisation	Day-time: teddies adopt their poses. Visitors to the museum (teachers in role – different hats) stare, giggle, point at them.
discussion	Out of role: how did they feel being stared at? Did anyone like it? Who in real life might like to be stared at? (Pop stars? etc.). Who might not like being stared at?
teacher in role	Night time (turn out lights – tension of contrast!): owner pleased to see her teddies. But. . .she has bad news: she must sell the museum (no one likes teddies any more). The new owner is visiting tomorrow. . .I don't know what her plans for you lot are. . .Reactions of group?

I N T E R V E N T I O N   P H A S E

?   ?   ?   ?

What Happened

This lesson followed a previous session on the theme of toys. This group of Year 1 and 2 mainstream infants had poor social skills, low self-esteem, and presenting behavioural difficulties; many had identified special educational needs and several were statemented. I would stick with relatively static strategies (control device!). In fact, the drama all happened in one corner of the room. The pupils had been highly motivated by a previous drama about teddies, so I decided to develop the theme and also hand over more responsibility for the direction of the drama. The lesson could lead to discussion on treatment of the elderly and respect despite appearances, which had really been explored analogously in this drama.

	DIAGNOSTIC PHASE
tableaux	I was surprised how well they coped. I kept it brief (so that they did not lose sight of the focus) and counted them in : 1, 2, 3. . . freeze. They were inventive, imaginative and fully in
questioning	control, and answered my questions with serious conviction. The lesson proceeded according to plan.
teacher in role	As the owner of the museum, I was almost taken aback by their warmth as they greeted me that night! I asked them about their day. . .one boy said there had only been two visitors all day. They were devastated at the bad news, and insisted they come with me. I told them they couldn't possibly: I could only afford to live in a very small place, and explained how I had become poor – people just did not want to spend money on coming to see old teddy bears any more; they were more interested in Teenage Mutant Hero Turtles. This prompted momentary contemplation! I told them about the new owner visiting the next day – they did not like this at all.
improvisation	They were angry and decided she must be horrid, even though I told them I didn't know anything about her. They wanted to make themselves look as nasty as possible for her. I did not attempt to persuade the pupils to do otherwise at this stage. I had made one attempt to encourage them to remain open-minded, but their ideas was fixed. This can be characteristic of many pupils with special educational needs: it is as if they lack the mental agility to think laterally and imagine the implications of following a different tack. *It was better to follow their initiative, and lead them to discover the logical implications of their behaviour.*

	INTERVENTION PHASE
teacher in role	The teddies adopted ghastly poses (they found it difficult to remain silent too!) as the new owner visited the next day. She commented how horrid the teddies looked – she'd be throwing them out straightaway.
narrative link	I moved the drama on to later that evening: the old owner had come to say 'Good'bye'.
teacher in role	The teddies were now subdued. Could they think of a way to save themselves? Tell about the secret – these were special teddies, even though they didn't look it?
writing reflection	They were to each write about what happened to the teddy they had played.

Partially-planned lesson *'THE FACTORY'* **Theme: WORLD OF WORK**

Aims: to consider aspects of factory life; to consider notions of 'responsibility' for oneself and others.

Staff: two to take roles (one taking both roles is possible, switching roles and props).

drama game	**TOPIC** Play warm up game: robot to bear down on pupil – get rid of it by shouting the name of someone else, to make robot change direction. Then ask where do we find robots? Let's find out!

↓

drama exercise discussion use of space teacher in role	**INITIATION PHASE** What is the machine like that makes them? Some pupils to be parts of the machine, others to work those bits; the rest to make the noises. How long can we do this without getting bored? (Put up hand when fed up). What must it be like in the factory? (Noisy? Boring? etc.). Rearrange furniture to create factory floor. What is the boss like? (preparation for teacher in role) – install in 'office'. Tell group that in a moment our drama will begin. Enter in role, brandishing newspaper: jobs have been advertised in the factory – we need the work (why do we need money?) Let's apply!

↓

drama exercise teacher in role rehearsal narrative link use of space teacher in role theatre structured play	**DIAGNOSTIC PHASE** Pupils to phone factory to arrange interview. Boss to be brisk and not tolerate dithering or sloppiness. Practise interview technique as group, advising each other on appropriate strategies. Move drama on in time: it is now the day of the interview. Rearrange chairs to represent waiting area outside office. Pupils to be interviewed briefly one at a time, and pushed through role as necessary towards appropriate behaviour. (They are all taken on once the boss is satisfied). Workers arrive for day-shift: check in and are allotted to a machine. Boss goes round questioning workers about their tasks (focus attention, deepen belief), and ensuring appropriate attitude to the task. (Attitudes of pupils? Learning area?).

report that
products are
faulty?

'rush' expected
– they must work
harder?

new worker
arrives – needs
training?

?

INTERVENTION PHASE

What Happened

This particular plan is highly versatile and adaptable across the age and ability range. On this occasion, I used it with 14–19–year old pupils with severe learning difficulties. The authoritative role of the boss put them under pressure to be on their mettle in a work situation. The inappropriate behaviour of the second role taken by a member of staff emphasized what was appropriate/inappropriate, the negative role illustrating the incongruity of inappropriate behaviour. This intriguing role also helped to capture their attention and keep them on task. The group had suggested the factory was a toy factory, although any place of work where they were part of a team could have done (farm, hotel, hospital, etc.).

improvisation	**DIAGNOSTIC PHASE** The workers meekly accepted work conditions, and set diligently about their tasks. One boy said he'd make us all a cup of tea. I seized his initiative: tea-break time! This of course meant digressing from my original plan, but his idea was appropriate and there was no reason not to go along with it. If I had stuck to my original plan, I would have risked losing their interest altogether, no longer *their* drama. The class had gathered in a corner, and were busy improvising a works cafeteria – the boy was organizing drinks for everyone. *I needed to deepen their belief and involvement. I acted promptly.*
teacher in role	I grabbed a hat in view of the group, and entered the cafeteria. Their attention was immediately riveted, and I asked them about work in the factory. They asked who I was – no one in particular, so I made up a name: 'Mr Wilson'. Some told me the work was boring, others that they enjoyed it; I consolidated their views. Did they think I could get a job in the factory? What was the boss like? What was the best way to deal with her? They gave me some tips.
theatre teacher in role	They watched attentively as I applied to the boss – she brought me to the factory floor, summoned the workers and told them they would have to train me, she was too busy. They each instructed me about the job they were doing and I seemed to be a willing learner. The atmosphere was calm and complacent. *I decided to challenge them further, as they needed to be put more on their mettle and have their sense of responsibility heightened.*
teacher in role	**INTERVENTION PHASE** I deliberately started messing around. Mixed reaction – some were incensed, others amused. *Their trainee was letting them down; they needed to take their responsibilities more seriously.* I made an excuse to leave.
teacher in role	The boss returned very angry. She had received complaints of faulty goods – who was to blame? (Would they blame me? – It didn't occur to them.) No one owned up, so she told them they had all been sacked and walked out.
teacher in role reflection	I entered as Mr Wilson (how would they react?) They were angry Out of role, we discussed issues of self-advocacy in the workplace.

Partially-planned lesson　　　*'NO ANSWER'*　　　**Theme: NEIGHBOURS**

Aims: to use appropriate initiative on behalf of neighbour in difficulty.
Staff: two to take roles.

Prescribed Drama

> **TOPIC**
> Play 'Roberta' (see level 2) – pupils in turn unwrap parcels containing items of clothing, and 'dress' Roberta. Let's find out more about Roberta.

use of space

teacher in role/mime

> **INITIATION PHASE**
> Make Roberta's house using masking tape on room-divider screen (outlines of windows, door, etc.). Pupils' initiatives – How many windows are there upstairs? Is there a number on the door? etc. Use masking tape or chalk to mark out Roberta's front garden (path, gate, fence, etc.).
>
> Explain that Roberta loves to do her garden. Put Roberta into the garden – she mimes activities. Can pupils guess what she is doing?

teacher in role/
theatre

narrative

narrative
drama exercise

tension

> **DIAGNOSTIC PHASE**
> Every morning people call at the house (who?) – second teacher in role as (eg, milkman) calls at house; they exchange 'Good morning' greetings. 'Rain or shine, Roberta is always in her garden'.
>
> 'One morning Roberta was not in her garden'. 'The milkman called. . .then the (?), then the (?) . . . but NO ANSWER'. Different pupils in turn to role-play (eg) postman, paper-boy, dustman, etc., and improvise calling at the house. (Reactions of pupils? Initiative?)

force entry?　　　　Roberta gone away?　　　　Roberta asleep?　　　　?

I N T E R V E N T I O N 　 P H A S E

76

What Happened

I have used the basic structure of this lesson several times previously – a house where people call and find no answer. On this occasion, I wanted to give this particular group of 8–10-year old pupils with severe learning difficulties (two with profound and multiple learning difficulties) a clear impression of the person who lived at the house, in order to provide a clear focus and sense of purpose. The Prescribed Drama activity allowed the character of Roberta to emerge gradually, allowing pupils time to 'catch up' with the significance of what was happening. It also successfully reached pupils at all levels of ability: it afforded important learning about drama conventions for some pupils, and a starting point for more open-ended drama for the others, whilst successfully embracing elements of cross-curricular learning for all of them (colours, conceptual skills, fine-motor skills, etc.). The drama particularly came alive at the point where Roberta entered the 'set' that the pupils had created for her.

theatre
–mime

Prescribed Drama
improvisation

teacher in role

DIAGNOSTIC PHASE
They watched attentively as she tended her garden. None of the pupils attempted to take charge of the drama at the point where several role-played callers at the house, although they had used some initiative: ringing the doorbell a second time, looking through a downstairs window. 'Do you think we should do something?', I prompted, 'Go and see', one girl replied. This was a popular suggestion – I needed to prevent them superficially rushing onwards, and to deepen their involvement in the drama. I slowed them down by playing 'Crossing the Road', (see level 1), which appealed at many levels of ability, as well as reinforcing road safety.
On arriving safely at the house, they began peering in at the windows, and rushing round the back. 'She's dead!', one boy exclaimed. Roberta had taken the initiative to lie down, and had decided to 'save' the drama for me – 'Help, help!', she was calling weakly! In fact, we could have followed the boy's idea, and checked for signs of life – science across the curriculum. They decided she needed medical help: *a 'learning area' – how to summon medical assistance if a neighbour is in difficulty.*

rehearsal
pairs improvisation

small group
improvisations

reflection

INTERVENTION PHASE
We practised what to dial and what to say to the hospital, before two pupils improvised the 'phone call', one taking the role of a member of the hospital staff.
Half carefully escorted Roberta to hospital in the 'ambulance' (elevating the status of one of the wheelchairs).
The rest of us decided we would visit her, taking some flowers from her garden, in the 'car' (the other wheelchair). Roberta was delighted and thanked us all: she was now much better.
Out of role, we discussed how we had summoned help, and what to do in real life if we thought a neighbour might be in difficulty.

Open lesson   *'PIRATES'*   **Theme: INVADERS AND SETTLERS**

Aims: to consider strategies for survival; to reflect on the value of human life with respect for all individuals.

Staff: two both to take roles; one swapping roles (switching props) is possible.

drama game

> **TOPIC**
> Play 'Pirate Chief' drama game as warm-up. Pupil (pirate chief) stands on chair in centre of circle. Group cluster round, passing bunch of keys secretly behind backs. Chant:
> *I am the pirate chief, I am the pirate chief,*
> *I'm standing on my treasure chest and*
> *One of you's got the keys.*
> If pirate chief guesses correctly, he or she chases that person round the back of the circle, and they become the pirate chief.

discussion

> Invite pupils to do drama about pirates. Do the pupils want to? (Be prepared to change tack if not!)

action replay?
ritual/song?

> **INITIATION PHASE**
> Ask pupils to suggest starting-point: pirates washed ashore? song round campfire? (ritual); listen to individual survival stories? Establish roles, where they are and what they are doing.

D I A G N O S T I C   P H A S E

teacher in role   This could be the mysterious 'island of treasure' – what do they think that means? What do they think we should do?

Prioritize survival?   Exploration of island? Treasure. . .?   Confrontation with islander?   ?

I N T E R V E N T I O N   P H A S E

What Happened

This was the final session of three with this group of junior mainstream primary school pupils. Their teacher had been concerned at the 'social health' of the group, particularly three statemented pupils integrated from a learning support centre who were stigmatized by the others. Over the previous two sessions, a strong group feeling had emerged with evidence of more positive group dynamics. As a class, I felt they were now ready to handle all decisions concerning the direction of the drama, and I would look to give it their play structure, depth and purpose in process. By the end of the session, we had come full circle, as in role, they experienced and respected the frustration of those who cope with an affliction. This led to further discussion out of role about disability issues.

song	**INITIATION PHASE** They decided to resume as pirates round the flag, and sang the Pirate Song.
ritual	We raised our palms in a 'Black spot' salute to reinforce a sense of 'group'.

theatre	*DIAGNOSTIC PHASE* Pirates then individually related accounts of their survival from the battle and shipwreck.
teacher in role	I then slowly took off my Pirate Chief headband and lay it in the circle – I had let them all down, and could no longer be their leader (reactions?)
tension	They insisted I carried on; I responded to their faith in me, and resolved to be 'democratic'. What were we to do? (Conscious abdication of responsibility for the direction of the drama).
discussion	We chalked options on a nearby 'rock' (blackboard!) and voted. Surprisingly, the majority wanted to stay put, not go exploring, seek the treasure or build a boat!
rehearsed improvisation	I asked them to show how the pirates obtained basic necessities: water, food, shelter and clothing.
questioning narrative	We watched each group in turn; the pupils could freeze the action at any moment to question the pirates. I then reported that before long some reported strange noises coming from a cave. . . *I was looking for a situation to confront their attitudes to people that were 'different'. . .*

movement	*INTERVENTION PHASE* Half the group made interesting shapes for the rest to wriggle through as the pirates explored the wooded island.
teacher in role	When they reached the 'cave', the islander appeared (wearing dramatic mask), brandishing a casket (reactions?). The pupils were very excited at this strong visual image – tension was high. She did not speak, but appeared to be offering the casket. They were sneering and snatched at it eagerly. . . the islander's silence broke: she laughed loudly and told them that as the new possessors of the casket, they would now be stricken with the 'curse of frozen tongue'.
narrative drama exercise/pairs reflection	'Two years later, the pirates were back home'. One ex-pirate was attempting to tell a friend an adventure, by signing only.

Open Lesson   *'THEME PARK'*   **Theme: THE ENVIRONMENT**

Aims: to consider channels for making a formal protest; to explore environmental issues involved
in the creation of theme parks.

Staff: three to take roles (two would be enough, by changing role and switching hats).

stimulus

> *TOPIC*
> Protest posters that the pupils had prepared before the lesson. Posters to be used as integral props for the drama (already agreed with the pupils).

discussion

> *INITIATION PHASE*
> Negotiate starting point for the drama with the pupils. How do the pupils want to begin: see the effect posters have on villagers? Meeting to decide course of action? Establish who they are, where they are and what they are doing. . .

D I A G N O S T I C   P H A S E

petition?   check planning permission?   demonstration?   ?

I N T E R V E N T I O N   P H A S E

80

What Happened

This lesson was the continuation of a drama begun a week previously with this group of 11–12–year old pupils with moderate learning difficulties. As woodland workers, their livelihood had been put under threat by the plans of a wealthy new landowner to develop a theme park. They had demonstrated considerable social maturity and were passionately motivated by the issues involved. This had surprised me – I was prepared for some ambivalence over the proposed creation of a theme park. I wanted them to negotiate all decisions from the outset, taking full responsibility for the drama.

small group improvisations	**INITIATION PHASE** The pupils briefly improvised scenes in the households as posters arrived advising of the proposed theme park and inviting villagers to a meeting.
teacher in role meeting small group improvisations writing theatre meeting	**DIAGNOSTIC PHASE** Head of local Residents' Association welcomed everyone and invited responses to the proposed theme park and suggestions for a course of action (consolidating views and attitudes). A list of possible strategies was drawn up and an action committee was formed to look into them ready for a follow-up meeting the next week. They worked at their assigned tasks: enquiring about planning permission at the local council (had it been granted?); drafting a formal letter to the developer Lady Mainwaring; forming a petition; putting up protest signs and fly-posters around the village. We eavesdropped on each in turn. Each group then summarized where they had got to (again to consolidate developments in the drama). The pupils were fairly complacent with their efforts; I perceived a need to respond with a greater sense of urgency. *Here was a learning area: how to lodge a formal protest effectively.*
teacher in role tension narrative ritual teacher in role questioning tableau drama ex. teacher in role art and design reflection	**INTERVENTION PHASE** I handed over a letter; tension was high as the head of the Resident's Association opened it and slowly read it: it was from Lady Mainwaring – their efforts were in vain, the contractors would be moving in next week. The pupils were incensed. We negotiated how to step up their action: involve the press, banners, TV and radio. They opted for a demonstration. I moved the drama on to the day of the demonstration. The pupils spontaneously reached for their posters and assembled – they broke into a chant: 'Save our trees'. As a TV reporter, I consolidated the drama, speaking to an imaginary camera and interviewing the protesters; they posed for a photo for the newspapers – could they invent a headline or caption? They heatedly challenged Lady Mainwaring, who said she might compromise. Interestingly, the pupils were suspicious and did not believe her! Could they design a park for all tastes that would satisfy all interests?

Open lesson   *'TEAMWORK'*   **Theme: WORLD OF WORK**

Aims: to consider skill and responsibility associated with professional jobs; to consider jobs involving interdependence within a team.

Staff: one to work in role.

theatre

> *TOPIC*
> Teacher begins to demonstrate practical skill (eg, moving someone carefully) on pupil lying on floor. Can group think of situation where people might have to do this? Negotiate a consensus where various jobs can be accommodated in a particular context, eg, hospital, hotel, etc.

use of space

drama exercises

structured play

> *INITIATION PHASE*
> Negotiate the 'playing area' (rearrange furniture? demarcate areas?).
>
> Establish everyone in role (test out suitability? interview?).
>
> Establish routines of chosen job/task.

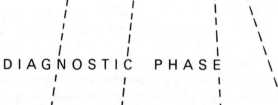

D I A G N O S T I C   P H A S E

Insist on commitment and serious attitude – deepen belief and engagement through challenges.

Look out for 'learning area' or problem to be resolved.

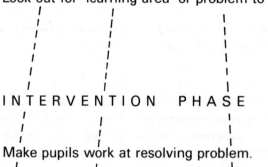

I N T E R V E N T I O N   P H A S E

Make pupils work at resolving problem.

What Happened

This skeleton lesson plan is extremely useful and adaptable. I was heartily glad I remembered it on this particular occasion, when opportunity for drama arose quite spontaneously and unexpectedly with this particularly volatile group of 7–8-year old pupils with moderate learning difficulties! Their teacher was discussing an aspect of caring for others, and was demonstrating a teaching point on a pupil, whom she had asked to lie down. This instantly caught their imagination: some leaped to their feet as 'nurses and doctors' in make-believe centred around the apparently injured pupil on the floor. I stepped in to endeavour to give this structure and purpose. . . they needed to slow down and consider the training and hard work involved in caring for a patient skilfully, and to be more aware of the interdependence of medical staff so that they would begin to cooperate and work together. This was a possible 'learning area', although I would have to remain flexible: something else might arise as the drama got more underway (Breaking bad news? Abuse of status?).

teacher in role (high status)	**INITIATION PHASE** I called the pupils back to their circle of seats. I asked if I could join in: when I next spoke to them, I would be pretending to be somebody else. I greeted them file in hand, as the boss and used the role to 'set frame': 'You must be the new people who want to work in this hospital'.
teacher in role use of space	**DIAGNOSTIC PHASE** They listened, but did not show initiative. I carried on, reading from an imaginary list of jobs, which would enable them to select a role that appealed: 'Let me see. . . We have some nurses, who are they please? Thank you'. By now they were beginning to suggest their roles. I then dropped role momentarily to organize the space for the drama with the pupils: the 'ambulance' and various parts of the room as areas on the 'ward'. The team were itching to get to work. *I needed to slow them down, and deepen their belief and understanding of the seriousness of their jobs.*
teacher in role rehearsal structured play talkover teacher in role improvisation art reflection	**INTERVENTION PHASE** I insisted they demonstrate their skills, so that I could be sure I had the very best team, before allowing them onto the ward. This created a sense of urgency to 'get it right'; the pupils could also practise skills they would need later on in the drama. I then established them on the 'ward' and in the 'ambulance', questioning them in role about their work to maintain their belief. The hospital tannoy announced a new patient was arriving on the casualty ward. Under the boss, they began to cooperate with some awareness of each other's roles, and dealt with the new patient with relatively quiet efficiency! Out of role, the pupils drew a picture about the drama, showing how everyone involved helped to make the patient better.

Bibliography

Arts Council of GB (1992) *Drama in Schools,* London: Arts Council of GB.

Baldwin, P. (1991) *Stimulating Drama,* Norwich: Norfolk Educational Press.

Bolton, G. (1979) *Towards a Theory of Drama in Education,* London: Longman.

Bolton, G. (1984) *Drama as Education,* London: Longman.

Bolton, G. (1992) *New Perspectives on Classroom Drama,* Padstow: Simon & Schuster.

Cattanach, A. (1992) *Drama for People with Special Needs,* London: A & C Black.

Davies, G. (1983) *Practical Primary Drama,* London: Heinemann Educational Books.

DES/WO (1990) *English in the National Curriculum,* No. 2 (Statutory Order for English), London: HMSO.

DFE (1993) *English for Ages 5-16 (1993): Proposals of the Secretary of State for Education and the Secretary of State for Wales,* London: HMSO.

Durham University Advanced Diploma Students (1982) 'Dramatic tension', *London Drama,* 6, 6, 16–17.

Gilham, G. (1974) 'Condercum school report', unpublished paper, Newcastle: Newcastle-upon-Tyne LEA.

Heathcote, D. (1976) in Wagner, B.J., op cit.

Heathcote, D. (1984) in O'Neill, C. and Johnson, L. (eds), op cit.

Jennings, S. (1973) *Remedial Drama,* London: Pitman.

Jennings, S. (1981) 'Drama therapy: Origins and the physically disabled', in Schattner, G. and Courtney, R. (eds) *Drama in Therapy, Volume one: Children,* New York: Drama Book Specialists.

Kempe, A. (1991) 'Learning both ways', *British Journal of Special Education,* 18, 4, 137–9.

Kempe, A. (1992) 'Enthusiastic beginners', *Drama,* Journal of National Drama, 1, 1, 13–16.

Landy, M. (1987) 'A drama diet for all?', *Support for Learning,* 2, 3, 27–32.

McClintock, A. (1984) *Drama for Mentally-Handicapped Children,* London: Souvenir Press.

McGregor, L., Tate, M. and Robinson, K. (eds) (1977) *Learning through Drama,* London: Longman.

NCC (1990) *English: Non-Statutory Guidance,* York: NCC.

NCC (1991) *Drama in the National Curriculum* (poster), York: NCC.

Neelands, J. (1984) *Making Sense of Drama,* London: Heinemann.

Neelands, J. (1992) *Learning through Imagined Experience,* London: Hodder & Stoughton.

Neelands, J. with Goode, T. (ed.) (1990) *Structuring Drama Work,* Cambridge: Cambridge University Press.

OFSTED (1992) *Framework for the Inspection of Schools,* London: OFSTED.

O'Neill, C. and Johnson, L. (eds) (1984) *Dorothy Heathcote: Collected Writings on Education and Drama,* London: Hutchinson.

O'Neill, C. and Lambert, A. (eds) (1982) *Drama Structures,* London: Hutchinson.

Polanyi, M. (1958) *Personal Knowledge: Towards a Post-Critical Philosophy,* London: Routledge & Kegan Paul.

SCDC – The Arts in Schools Project (1987) *A Special Collaboration,* London: SCDC.

Sheppard, D. (1991) 'Developing drama and art in primary schools' in Sullivan, M. (ed.) *Supporting Change and Development in the Primary School,* Harlow: Longman.

Sherborne, V. (1990) *Developmental Movement for Children,* Cambridge: Cambridge University Press.

Taylor, J. (1983) 'Helter Skelter (Drama Games)', London: ILEA (unpublished)

Taylor, J. (1984) 'Steps to Drama', London: ILEA (unpublished).

Taylor, J. (1986a) 'Frankenstein's monster', *London Drama Magazine,* 7, 3, Autumn, 17–19.

Taylor, J. (1986b) 'Drama and special needs', London: ILEA (unpublished).

Tomlinson, R. (1982) *Disability, Theatre and Education,* London: Souvenir Press.

Wagner, B.J. (1976) *Dorothy Heathcote – Drama as a Learning Medium,* London: Hutchinson.

Ward, D. (1989) 'The arts and special needs', in Ross, M. (ed.) *The Claims of Feeling,* London: Falmer Press.

Warger, C. (1985) 'Making creative drama accessible to handicapped children', *Teaching Exceptional Children,* 17, 4, 288–93.